The Language that Remains

The Language that Remains

Time, History, Language

Giorgio Agamben

Translated by Scott Kirkland

polity

Originally published in Italian as *La lingua che resta: Il tempo, la storia, il linguaggio*

This book has been translated thanks to a translation grant awarded by the Italian Ministry of Foreign Affairs and International Cooperation / Questo libro è stato tradotto grazie a un contributo alla traduzione assegnato dal Ministero degli Affari Esteri e della Cooperazione Internazionale italiano.

Polity Press
65 Bridge Street
Cambridge CB2 1UR, UK

Polity Press
111 River Street
Hoboken, NJ 07030, USA

ISBN-13: 978-1-5095-7044-7 – hardback
ISBN-13: 978-1-5095-7045-4 – paperback

A catalogue record for this book is available from the British Library.

Library of Congress Control Number: 2026937121

Typeset in 11 on 14 pt Sabon
by Cheshire Typesetting Ltd, Cuddington, Cheshire
Printed and bound in Great Britain by Ashford Colour Ltd

For further information on Polity, visit our website:
politybooks.com

Contents

Translator's Note

Where possible I have worked with standard English editions of texts cited by the author. However, I have modified those translations on occasion to retain the sense of the Italian. I would like to thank the editor at Polity, Elise Heslinga, for her patience with me; my colleague and friend, Adam Kotsko, for his encouragement to undertake the translation; and my colleagues at Trinity College for creating a collegial and supportive environment where such academic endeavours are not only tolerated but encouraged.

I

Aion and *Chronos*: New Theses on the Concept of History

Nemo sibi persuadeat ... fieri posse ut accurata scientia ratio temporum comprehendatur quae profecto alucinatio est. [Let no one convince himself ... that it is possible to comprehend the exact scientific account of time, which is certainly a hallucination.]

Eusebius, *Chronicarum canonum libri duo*

Oh history, oh history, what are you?

G. E. Lessing, *Fifth Dialogue for Freemasons*

You know my ancient purpose: to find the saga of the history of the world.

L. von Ranke, *Über die Epochen der neueren Geschichte*

1. History, as we know and practise it, is an essentially Christian concept. 'Christianity', wrote Marc Bloch in that kind of spiritual testament that is the *Apologie pour l'histoire,* 'is a religion of historians. Other systems of religion have founded their beliefs and rites upon a mythology which is in some way outside human time; the sacred books of Christians are books of history and their liturgies commemorate, with the episodes of the

earthly life of a God, the glories of the Church and the saints. Christianity is historical in another way, perhaps even more profoundly: positioned between the Fall and Judgement, the destiny of humanity appears before its eyes as a long adventure, of which each individual life, each singular "pilgrimage", constitutes a reflection; it is in the duration – and, therefore, in history – that the central axis of every Christian meditation unfolds, the grand drama of Sin and Redemption' (Bloch, p. 38).

It is unsurprising, therefore, that history has for centuries been the province of monks and theologians. Even the method of historical philology was invented in the seventeenth century by a Benedictine monk, Jean Mabillon. When the Enlightenment took hold of it, the feeble resistance of theologians should have rendered historians more cautious. For history has become the Trojan horse which has penetrated the citadel of reason.

The feasts of the Christian liturgical calendar, such as Easter or Christmas, in this way entirely like civil holidays, first of all celebrate and commemorate historical facts and not meta-historical or legendary events. The resurrection of Christ, states the easter message of Benedict XVI in 2009, 'is not a theory, but a historical reality revealed by the man Jesus Christ through his "Passover" [. . .]. It is not a myth or a dream, not a vision or a utopia, not a fairy tale, but a singular and unrepeatable event'. The specificity of the Christian calendar is that it organizes historical time with reference to events which are themselves fully historical.

In stressing the theological signature of the modern conception of history, obviously we do not intend to deny that historical thought, as Mazzarino has demonstrated, was already born in Greece in the sixth century BCE, and that, therefore, too sharp a contraposition between ancient and modern history ought to be subject to limitations and reservations of various kinds; as ought to become clear in the course of reading, the opposition concerns a point that is precise yet not to be neglected: the constitution of the paradigm of historical time as such.

A clue to the theological signature which inheres in the concept of history as we know it is the double significance – both objective and subjective – of the term in modern languages: if *historia* designated in Greek only historical investigation, historiography and not its object, from a certain point onward the term homonymously refers to both the practice of the historian and the object on which he works, both the *historia rerum gestarum* and the *res gestae* (Toynbee noted rightly in this sense that Herodotus' title *hystories apodexis* ought to be translated as *The Exhibition of Inquiry*). But even this object, by reason of the theological signature that defines it, is then split in time into the purely quantitative series of events and the character that qualitatively constitutes them as 'historical' (from the theological perspective: profane history and the history of salvation, which attributes a significance and a direction to a time and events that are in themselves devoid of them; in its secularized version: the idea of progress and a meaning of history). When Hegel writes that the two meanings of the term 'history' refer to a unity which is not just external contingency, and that 'the narration of history makes its appearance contemporaneously with the actual historical deeds and events: a single foundation makes both arise' (Hegel, p. 54), the presupposed foundation here is the theological idea according to which history is the objective realization of the divine spirit. As for the passage from Polybius (*Universal History*, I, 3, 4), in which the term *historia* designates both the *res gestae* and the *historia rerum gestarum*, it needs to be considered more attentively: 'From these times (*kairon*) it occurred as if (*oionei*) *historia* took on the form of a body (*somatoeide*) and the Italian and Libyan practices were intertwined (*symplekesthai*) with those of Asia and the Greeks, producing a reference (*anaphora*) of all towards a single end (*pros en telos*)'. Here, in reality, the 'single *telos*' and the 'as if it became a body' refer, not to objective history, but to the investigation (*historia*) of the historian: the unity of the narration is decisive and not the constitution of a single historical time.

3

2. 'In the forty-second year of the reign of Augustus, twenty-eight years after the subjection of Egypt and the death of Antony and Cleopatra, when the dominion of Ptolemy over Egypt ended, our Lord and Saviour Jesus Christ was born in Bethlehem of Judea, at the moment of the first census, according to the prophecy'. This passage from the *Ecclesiastical Histories* of Eusebius (I, VI) is important not only because it establishes the chronological dating of the birth of Christ, but also, and primarily, because it confers upon that event a particular connotation, which would change the meaning of every event in the history of humanity. Whoever wishes to commit to writing the history of the Christian community, writes Eusebius, must put it in relation to the beginning of the 'economy of Christ', that is, to the divine plan for the redemption of humanity. To conceive of the series of historical events as a divine *oikonomia* (in the words of Augustine, as *historia dispensationis temporalis divinae providentiae*) means in fact to constitute it as a coherent whole endowed with intelligible sense. To fix a chronology and, at the same time, to attribute, by the very fact that one is situated in them, a significance to the events which it enables to date: it is only the conjunction of these two elements that defines Christian history with regard to that of classical history. From now on, to date – that is, to construct a continuous temporal framework – means to give sense, and to give sense means to date.

In this context that assertion – otherwise incomprehensible – of the name of the prefect of Judea, Pontius Pilate, in the Nicene-Constantinopolitan creed, in which the Fathers summarized the essence of the Christian faith, is explained. It was a question of historically dating the events of the crucifixion and, simultaneously, of inserting history into the economy of salvation.

In his *Chronographia,* composed between 303 and 326, Eusebius inserted the *Canones*, a synchronic table of biblical history and pagan history from the time of Abraham to the birth of Christ. The original Greek is lost, but the Latin version of Jerome (finished circa 381) formed the basis of all subsequent Latin chronicling. It recounts 5,198 years until the birth of Christ and, unlike the earlier chronographies of Hippolytus and Julius Africanus, it does not contain a reference to the end of time. For this reason it could be said that Eusebius liberated the Christian chronicle from chiliasm (Von den Brincken, *passim*).

3. Towards the middle of the third century CE, Julius Africanus composed in Greek in Palestine the six books of the *Chronographiai*, in which he proposed to articulate chronologically the history of humanity from the creation of Adam to the coming of Christ. It is from this perspective that he had to succeed in synchronizing the data of the biblical chronologies with that of Hellenistic historiography marked by Olympiads. 'Until the Olympics', he writes, 'the Greeks have nothing which is precise, everything is mixed with something else and there is no agreement. The Olympiads are given careful analysis by many, on the basis of the fact that the Greeks divide their accounts not according to broad periods of time, but into four-year periods. For this reason, I will treat only briefly a selection of the most famous mythical histories (*mythodeis historiai*) leading to the first Olympiad. I will pair the subsequent events each according to its time (*syzeyxas katà chronon ecastas*), the events of the history of the Jews with that of the Greeks, and in so doing I will inquire into the history of

the Jews, placing it in relation (*ephaptomoenos*) to the history of the Greeks. In so doing I will connect them harmoniously (*epharmoso*). I will achieve my purpose, if, to the extent that I deal with an action of the Jews, which I will investigate as contemporaneous (*homochronou*) with an action of the Greeks, I succeed in demonstrating, through additions and deletions, which of the Greeks or the Persians is contemporaneous (*synchronisen*) with the events of the Jews'.

4. Mazzarino has demonstrated that the classical conception of historical time was especially articulated through synchronizations ('a coordinate of straight horizontal lines [. . .] with straight vertical lines' (Mazzarino 1966, II.2, p. 439), and the chronography of Africanus would seem to follow the same paradigm. The true novelty of the *Chronographiai* is, however, that their purpose is not to narrate the history of this or that people, or of the various peoples as a whole, as is the case in Hellenistic universal histories, rather it is to Christianize time, that is, to constitute historical time itself as universal Christian time, removing it, in this way, from the mythologemes and incompleteness of preceding chronologies. The expression 'historical time', here implicitly contrasted with 'mythical stories', should be understood in a technical sense. It has reference to the distinction, already formulated by Varro, between the unknowable time of the beginning of humanity (*quod propter ignorantiam vocatur 'adelon'*), until the time of the first Olympiad, which is called 'mythic' (*mythikon* – the *mythodeis historiai* of Africanus), *quia multa in eo fabulosa referuntur*, and, finally, the succeeding time, which is called 'historical'

(*quod dicitur 'historikon', quia res in eo gestae veris historiis continentur*). Commenting on this tripartition, a contemporary of Africanus, Censorinus, writes that 'if it were possible to have knowledge of the origins of the world, we would begin from there' (*et si origo mundi in hominum notitiam venisset, inde exordium sumeremus*: Censorinus, *De die natali*, 21, I). Thanks to the Genesis narrative, Africanus knows that he can have this knowledge, and can, therefore, synchronizing the story of the Hebrews with that of the Greeks, transform all time into historical time.

We then understand the decisive issue at stake in the *Chronographiai*: the *historikon* ceases to be – as it was again in Varro and Censorinus – an *intervallum temporis* alongside unknowable time and mythical time, and coincides now with the time of the history of the world. For this, when, two centuries later, Philip of Side composed his *Christianiké historia*, which encompasses everything of the history of humanity in its 36 books, from Adam to his present, the title does not refer obviously to the history of Christians: history – and this is the first accomplishment of the new chronology – is in itself constitutively homogeneous and 'Christian'. Chronography, the *temporis universi ratio*, without which, according to Bodin, 'no fruit can be gathered from history', is the passage through which theology penetrated historical reason.

It was F. Jacoby (Jacoby, pp. 80–123) who coined the expression *spatium historicum* to designate the object of ancient historiography as distinct from mythical accounts. As always, caution is required when projecting modern terminology (even if dressed up in Latin) onto classical authors. The decisive testimony here is Diodorus (IV, 1.3) regarding Ephorus of Cumae:

'Ephorus of Cumae, a student of Isocrates, engaged in the editing of the common actions (*koinas praxeis* – not properly "universal history", as it is sometimes translated, but the actions of single peoples located with each other in a synchronic relation), omitted (*yperebe*) ancient mythologies and made the return of the Heraclids the *arke tes historias*'. What is essential here is the problem of the *arche*, of the point from which historical narration begins, and not, as it will be for Christian authors, the constitution of a particular object, historical time, which goes back in time to include what would have appeared to antique historians as *archaiai mythologiai.*

In the *Methodus ad historiarum cognitionem* of Bodin (1650), the theological root of historical knowledge remains evident. History is threefold: human, natural and divine, but true historical knowledge results only from their articulation, in which divine history is granted a privileged rank (*adipiscendi magnum est ab historia triplici adiumentum, maxime vero a divina*). There the necessity of ordering time in a chronology is, for this reason, reiterated with force: *sine temporum ratione vix ullos ab historia decerpi fructus* (ch. viii). This seventeenth-century reflection on history did nothing but reiterate an exigency which had already been significantly and clearly expressed at the beginning of the patristics: 'where there is not a coherent order of time', we read in the *Oratio ad Graecos* of Tatian, 'there can be no true history', and Jerome, in the prologue to the *Canones* of Eusebius, defined chronology as 'the soul of history' (Scaligero must have called this definition to mind when he wrote, always with reference to Eusebius, that 'without chronology history cannot breathe' (*sine chronologia historia non spirat*).

5. Julius Africanus is the first to adopt the schema of the biblical hexameron without reservation. The idea of assuming the six days of creation as a paradigm for calculating the hexamillennial ages of the world was present already in Hippolytus' *Commentary on Daniel* and in Irenaeus, and, before them, in Jewish apocalypticism. But, while in these authors the hexamillennial

form took an essentially eschatological meaning, Julius Africanus simply makes it the foundation of a historical chronography. Basing it on the scriptural testimony according to which 'with the Lord one day is like a thousand years, and a thousand years like one day' (2 Peter 3:8; cf. Psalms 89 (90):4), he calculates the duration of the history of humanity at 6,000 years, and places the incarnation in the year 5500, in the middle of the sixth day, leaving, therefore, 500 years from that moment until the Parousia. It is essential for him that the cosmic hexameron permits the constitution of a universal history, understood as an absolute historical time, theologically constituted and oriented, through a beginning and an end, according to the divine plan of salvation: eschatology serves to found history, and not only to signal its end.

The peculiarity of Christian time is that it entails an event, the incarnation or resurrection of Christ, which in some way signals a second beginning and an anticipation of the *eschaton*, in which time itself transforms and contracts as it begins to end. And this event, though situated at the centre and not at the beginning of chronology, signals the origin of the calculation, necessitating a singular retroactive dating from it that also acts upon the preceding time, because every instant and every event of that earlier time, now constituted as time under the law in relation to time under grace, enters into a typological or figural relation with the coming of the messiah. The messianic event, though being, as with all others, a historical fact, is distinguished from them in that it confers on them their true meaning, signified by the dating *ante* or *post Christum natum*.

Only the second coming of Christ, the *parousia*, marks the end of time in the chronological sense. The duration of this interval, which in the expectation of the first communities was necessarily brief, has been prolonged indefinitely, and the Church, in its progressive neutralization of the eschatological, has ended by flattening messianic time onto infinite chronological historical time. Hence the recurring vindication of messianic time in chiliastic movements and among thinkers who, like Benjamin, forcefully affirm its heterogeneity with respect to chronological time, of which it constitutes an arrest and an interruption.

6. *Dionysius Exiguus*, Dionysius the Humble, a Scythian monk active in Rome in the first half of the sixth century, composed a table of Easter dates for a period of 95 years. This was conceived as a continuation of a previous list which calculated the years, according to Egyptian custom, from Diocletian's imperial accession and ending with the year 247 from that date. Instead of beginning his table with the year 248 of the Diocletian era, Dionysius decided to number the years from the incarnation of Christ. 'We refuse', writes Dionysius, 'to bind our calculations to the memory of that impious emperor; we have chosen, instead, to designate the periods of the years from the beginning of the incarnation of our Lord Jesus Christ, so that the beginning of our hope might become more evident to us and the cause of the salvation of humanity, that is, the passion of the Redeemer, might become more resplendent'. The year 248 of the Diocletian calendar thereby became the year 532 *Domini nostri Jesu Christi*.

Dionysius certainly could not have imagined that his decision would become the foundation of a new chronology that would progressively impose itself throughout most parts of the world. Two centuries later, the Venerable Bede admitted Dionysian dating into his *The Reckoning of Time* and shortened the formula to *anno Domini*, which remains current today. Although, as has been noted, a year beginning with the Incarnation should have commenced on March 25, that is, nine months before the nativity of Christ, a week before January 1, Bede preferred to align his chronology with the Julian calendar, which, like our calendar, commences on January 1.

7. All chronologies somehow resemble each other. Scholars have noted that some of the elements which define Christian chronographies are previously found in Greek chronologies, such as the *Marmor Parium* and the *Chronicon Romanum* and the Hellenistic attempts to construct a universal history, such as the *Chronographiai* of Eratosthenes and the *Chronica* of Apollodorus composed in iambic trimeter. In this sense, Mazzarino has observed that the contraposition, which can be traced back to Augustine, between pagan circular time and Christian linear time is not necessarily absolute, and that elements of circularity are present in the Christian conception of time just as linear elements are in the classical conception. And if Mazzarino's genealogy of Greek historical thought, which traces back to Epimenides' 'prophecy on the past' and the necessity to purify the present through knowledge of the past, is correct, then Christian history as an economy of salvation is, likewise, not absolutely new.

When investigating a historical paradigm, however, the accurate description of the structure is not sufficient; one must also understand the intention or strategic function for which it was conceived or used. Even conspicuous structural analogies can thus correspond to strategies that are completely different and even incompatible. Neither linear chronology nor the economy of salvation alone are sufficient to define Christian temporality: this is constituted only though their indissoluble conjunction, in which the historical-chronological element of dating immediately acquires theological value. Dionysius Exiguus' decision to take the birth of Christ as the beginning of his paschal calculation thus undoubtedly resembles that of the proconsul Paullus, governor of the Greek cities of Asia two centuries earlier, to consider the anniversary of Augustus as 'the beginning of all things'; but Paullus did not have in mind, as did the Christians who adopted Dionysius' dating as the basis for their calendar, a philosophy and theology of history.

It is appropriate to distinguish, from this perspective, political chronologies, relating to a magistrate in office, the reign of a sovereign or the founding of a city, and cultic chronologies which are intended to regulate the celebration of religious festivals, from theological-philosophical chronologies, which imply a philosophy of history.

Thus in Athens there was a cultic calendar of twelve lunar months, which had the aim of regulating the celebration of the religious festivals, and a political calendar of ten months, in which the dates were calculated from the name of the representative of the ten tribes who, at that time, occupied the prytany (in inscriptions from the fifth century CE, we find formulas of this type: 'It was decided by the *Boulé* and the people, when Aigeis occupied the prytany and Neocles was secretary . . .'). The Roman dating *ad urbe condita*, the Macedonian dating from the death of Alexander and the Olympic era also undoubtedly have a political significance. Even in the Christian ambit, there are chronologies that have a purely cultic or political function (such as the previously cited era of Diocletian, used for the most part among Christians in Egypt) or even apologetic, such as those of Theophilus and Clement of Alexandria, which essentially aimed at proving the greater antiquity of Moses relative to the Greeks (who derived their wisdom from him).

The chronology that Christianity has passed on to modernity is, by contrast, a theological-philosophical chronology, because, although it contains elements present in political and cultural chronologies, it integrates them into the perspective of a universal history, whose intelligibility depends exclusively on the divine economy of salvation. Even those scholars who emphasize Africanus' debt to his predecessors must then admit (Burgess, pp. 35–7) that, although he takes up the apologetic arguments of Clement and Theophilus, Africanus shifts apologetic chronographies to a new horizon. If, on the one hand, he seems to bring Christian chronography back to the secular Hellenistic model, on the other, 'he was not writing Greek, Roman, Egyptian, Babylonian, Jewish or Tyrian history, as was the case with his predecessors, but Christian history, that is, history from a Christian perspective, not a history of the Church' (ibid., p. 37). He 'forces Christian chronography to adopt the method and structure' of secular historiography (ibid., p. 38), but the purpose of this shift is to construct a universal Christian history, beginning with creation and ending with the end of the world. That is to say, it is a question of situating historiographical materials, the *historoumena*, within the Christian chronographic architecture and, vice versa, of inscribing the economy of salvation in a historical context. Africanus creates, that is, a Christian *time*; his specific achievement is not the construction of a chronology for Christian historiography, but rather the *Christianization of time* – or, if you will, the temporalization of Christianity – as the condition of possibility of a universal history.

8. Mazzarino has observed that Indo-European languages have two families of terms to express time: one that derives from the Latin *saeculum* and the Greek *chronos*, which indicates countable time, and another that derives from the Latin *aevum* and the Greek *aion*, which correspond to lived time. '*Chronos* and *Aion* prevailed according to whether, in the intuition of time, the aspect of arithmetical succession or that of vitality implicit in the temporality itself was stressed' (Mazzarino III, p. 454). The opposition is, in reality, also between time and motion (*chronos*) and immobile

time (*aion*, *kairos*). So it is that in Plato's *Timaeus*, *chronos*, countable time, is defined as a moving image of *aion*, eternal and undatable time, and, in Aristotle, *chronos* is the number of movement, whereas *aion* is the completion that embraces the *chronos* of every man.

In the classical world, at least until Plotinus, it was essential that the two figures of time remain distinct and heterogeneous. For Christianity, however, it was decisive to think of their intersection. *Chronos*, countable historical time, is not only an image of eternity: it is the realization of the eternal plan, of the 'mystery' of salvation decided by God. The specific achievement of Christian theology is, in this sense, the articulation of *chronos* and *aion*, of countable time and eternity, in an 'economy'. Origen can thus conceive of history as a 'mysterious economy', through which certain mysteries are revealed to those who know how to investigate them historically (Origen, p. 303). The point at which the two times coincide is the event of the incarnation, which initiates the *eschaton*, 'the end time' in which all times find their completion. The time before the eschatological time is, in fact, a constitutively unfinished time, which finds its only meaning in being a *typos* and allegory of the time that is fulfilled in Christ. In the Christian conception of history, eschatology not only has a soteriological meaning, but also serves as the paradigm that unites the two figures of time.

The historical machine of modernity is, therefore, a bipolar machine, founded on the tension and articulation of two heterogeneous times: *chronos* and *aion*, quantitative and countable time, and qualitative and uncountable time, chronological time and eschatological time. From time to time, one pole may prevail over the other, but if, as has happened in modernity, one of the poles – *aion* – is removed, the historical-theological machine can no longer function. Just as in first philosophy we speak of an ontological difference, we can call this division of historical time into two heterogeneous yet closely linked elements an 'eschatological difference'. According to the Freudian axiom of the return of the repressed in pathological forms, a theological signature does not cease to reappear in the historical practice of modernity. Eschatological aeonic time, which had been hastily set aside, reappears as an internal requirement of chronological time, which more or less unconsciously refers to an epochal principle that transcends it and without which it remains incomprehensible.

It is proper to 'aeonic' time to constitute a certain diachronic progression in a synchronic conceptual unity in order to allow for its comprehension. Since a purely quantitative temporal succession would be incomprehensible, we continue to articulate it qualitatively through categories such as 'medieval', 'modern', 'baroque', 'French Revolution', 'decadence', etc., so that understanding of history results from the dialectic between these chronological categories.

It is from this perspective that we should read the controversy between Mazzarino and Momigliano following the publication of the Sicilian historian's book *Between East and West* (1947). In his review, Momigliano reproaches Mazzarino for transforming 'phantom-problems' into historical reality. Only on the basis of improbable conjectures can the East and West, Asia and Greece, be presented as characters in a 'spiritual drama'. 'The eastern soul has had its time and with it the Greek soul [. . .]. Greeks and Asians no longer stand at the threshold of history' (Mazzarino 1989, p. 399). The expression 'at the threshold of history' is significant: East and West, as with all categories of the same kind that Mazzarino often uses, stand outside history properly understood. Rightly clarifying that, in reality, it is a 'methodological problem', Mazzarino reiterates that 'the East–West problem is central to the history of humanity' (ibid., p 407) and that what Momigliano calls 'phantom-problems' are, in fact, categories that cannot be eliminated from historical research. In the final analysis, what is at stake here is the contrast between aeonic conceptuality and chronological conceptuality, and the fact that it is not possible to completely eliminate the former from historiographical practice is proven by the fact that even a positive historian such as Momigliano does not hesitate to use it when he deems it necessary.

9. One of the most singular forms of this resurgence of aeonic time is the 'century'. We are so habituated to considering the division into centuries as normal that we forget that the concept of the century in this particular sense is a relatively recent creation, which appeared for the first time with Flacius Illyricus, a Protestant theologian of Istrian origin who, together with other reformed theologians published, between 1559 and 1574, a history of the Church divided into centuries or *centuriae* (*Ecclesiastica historia, integra Ecclesiae Christi ideam* [. . .] *secundum singulas centurias perspicuo ordine complectens*).

The example of the *centuriatores* – as they were initially ironically named – was only gradually established from the seventeenth century onwards; however, it is interesting to see how, already in their historiographical practice, the century gradually acquired an epochal value and designated a synchronic state rather than a simple diachronic series. As the scholar who reconstructed its genealogy observed, 'the calculation by centuries is based on the systematic elements of history and not chronological ones' (Burkhardt, p. 27). The question is theoretically relevant because the claim to transform mere numerical convention (the calculation of one hundred years) into a substantial reality is, obviously, devoid of any foundation. (That still today representatives of an academic discipline consider themselves to be scientific while declaring themselves specialists of the fifteenth or eighteenth centuries, only demonstrates the degree of epistemological irresponsibility prevalent in the human sciences.)

It has been observed that the *centuriatores*, so as to define the *Status Ecclesiae* in each of the centuries in which they articulated its history, use the expression *in hoc saeculo* or *in hac aetate* (also sometimes *hoc tempus*) and, in this way, seem to suggest the idea that the articulation by centuries corresponds to a substantial unity (a certain 'state of the Church', which is each time different: ibid., p. 22). But, in this way, they are merely repeating New Testament usage which contrasts the present aeon in a strongly epochal sense (*en to aion touto*, *in hoc seculo*, *hoc aion outos*, *hoc tempus*) with a future aeon. From the outset, the century as a historical unit bears within it a clear theological signature, which leads it to progressively assume the characteristics of those ages or epochs of the world, already familiar to the ancient world, which Christianity had inserted, in the form of the biblical hexameron, into an economy of salvation.

It is significant that in Egidio da Viterbo's *Historia viginti saeculorum* (1519), the twenty centuries in which he articulates the history of humanity are not periods of one hundred years, but have different durations each time: they are therefore still ages and not numerical entities. But even when, in following centuries, the century seems to become a neutral tool of calculation, it nonetheless remains a synchronous state of an aeonic nature and not a diachronic course. As Burkhardt's book clearly shows, calculation by centuries progressively transformed into a tool for organizing historical material, until it became the privileged device in post-Hegelian historiography for articulating history into epochs.

10. Flacius' invention of the century, in the first instance strongly opposed, eventually spread to every area of historical research, even if still in the course of the seventeenth century we find forms of historical writing, such as Leibniz's *Annales Imperii occidentis Brunsvicenses*, which do not make use of it. An important moment in this diffusion is the publication of the *Acta sanctorum in saeculorum classes distributa* by the Benedictines of Saint Mauro, led by Mabillon (1668–1701). Although here the 'first century' coincides with the sixth century following the birth of Christ (i.e., with the founding of the Benedictine order), the division into centuries is maintained unreservedly. Curiously Mabillon, who was the founder of historical diplomatics, also classifies the findings of his palaeographic science by the centuries. The examples of writing styles are then listed *in saeculorum classes*, as if each century corresponded to a certain *ductus* and a certain form of writing. In this way, the idea that the century was a reality and not an abstract numerical convention obtains a further, almost perceptible, consistency: each century seems to have its own graphological image, just as later it will have attributed an artistic style.

Exactly fifty years separate the publication of the *Acta Sanctorum*, the last great work of monastic philology, from the first edition of Voltaire's masterpiece of Enlightenment historiography, *Le siècle de Louis XIV*, which was to have a lasting influence on subsequent historiography. 'In Voltaire's concept of *siècle*', it has been written, 'the order of centuries, the dynastic period, and the epochal content overlap perfectly' (Burkhardt, p. 91). 'Le siècle que j'appelle de Louis XIV' is both a chronological century (which Voltaire dates from the founding of the *Académie* in 1635) and, as we read in the introduction, one of the four 'golden ages' of the world. The theological paradigm of the century thus reaches its full epochal significance in this book, in which the numerical convention claims to reflect a somewhat unified reality, and *chronos* immediately presents itself as an *aion*, an 'epoch' or 'historical aeon'.

It has been rightly observed that, once the articulation has been accepted by historiography for centuries, it ceases to be a perspective introduced into history *a posteriori*, but becomes the medium through which contemporary consciousness comprehends itself epochally ('Medium ihres epochalen Selbstverständnisses': ibid., p. 123).

When, in a poem that has been commented upon many times, Mandelstam addresses his own time, calling it 'My Age!' and comparing it to a beast with a broken spine (But your spine is cracked / my beautiful, pitiful, age. / With a dumb grimace, you writhe / look back, feebly, with cruel jaws / a creature, once supple and lithe, / at the tracks left by your paws), it is evident that he experiences it as a concrete reality through which he also understands himself. The poet, like the true historian, situates himself at the point of fracture in which *aion* and *chronos*, the epochal time of life and chronological time, seek to find their impossible articulation.

11. The more or less conscious connection between theology and history, between theological significance and chronological periodization, appears in all its complexity

in Leopold von Ranke – that is, precisely in the historian against whom Benjamin directs his critique of historicism, which claims to know the past 'as it actually was'. A reading of the introduction to the first lecture of *Über die Epochen der neueren Geschichte* (1854) is particularly instructive. Rejecting any idea of progress in history, Ranke here firmly distances himself from both Hegelian philosophy of history and Christian theology's history of salvation: 'If one were to argue', he writes, 'contradicting the ideas presented here, that progress consists in the fact that in every age the life of humanity is enhanced and that therefore each generation completely surpasses the previous one, which in this way is only the bearer of the next, this would imply an injustice on the part of the deity (*eine Ungerechtigkeit der Gottheit*). Such a mediating generation would have no meaning in itself, and would only make sense as a degree of the next generation and would therefore not be in immediate relation to the divine (*in unmittelbarem Bezug zum Göttlichen*). I affirm instead: every era is immediate with respect to God (*jede Epoche ist unmittelbar zu Gott*) and its value does not consist in what comes from it, but in its very existence, in its very self' (Ranke, p. 17).

It is striking that, in the very act of distancing his thinking from any philosophy of history, Ranke instead confirms its unmistakable theological signatures. These are manifest above all in the apocalyptic-messianic character of the theorem according to which every era is in immediate relation with God. This is what Marrou clearly understood, seeing in the theorem – which Benjamin certainly would not have disliked – the expression of the 'mysterious relationship that is established between time and eternity in the perspective of

Christian theology of history' (Marrou 1979, p. 74). In this, in fact, as we have seen, time is linear, but every point in it is in immediate relation to the coming of the messiah. Every generation, according to Ranke's image, is equidistant from eternity, because not only every era but every personal existence is immediately related to the end of time. 'For every civilization and every human generation, as for every living man, it must be recognized that its last and only day [. . .] is the Last Day [. . .]. All time takes on, from this perspective, an eschatological quality' (ibid.).

No less significant is the other theological signature, which means that, for Ranke, the series of historical events is composed, according to an intimate connection, in an epoch, and the series of epochs in turn draws a universal history. 'If we admit', he writes in a manuscript from the 1860s, 'that history cannot have the unity of a philosophical system, it is not without an intimate link (*innere Zusammenhang*) [. . .]. What has become is linked by a coherent link with what is becoming, but this link is not arbitrary; rather, it is always in a certain way and not in another. In any case, it is an object of knowledge. A longer series of events – one after another and side by side – joined together in this way forms a century, an epoch [. . .]. If we represent the series of centuries in this way, each in its original essence (*in seiner ursprünglichen Wesenheit*), all linked in themselves, then we will have before us a universal history (*Universalgeschichte*), from the beginning to the present day. Universal history comprehends the past life of humanity, not in individual relations and directions, but in its fullness and totality' (Ranke, pp. 6–7).

Once more, a paradigm linked to chronography and Christian theology determines the historian's gaze to the end of making him see a 'universal essence' and an 'intimate link' in what appears to be simply a numerical convention. As has been effectively observed, the calculation of centuries is a 'historiographical technique' whose essential function is the construction of epochs, in which 'the general representation of a historical process appears significantly connected with the series of centuries' (Burkhardt, p. 113).

It was a student of Ranke, Ottokar Lorenz, who attempted to found an epochal understanding of the centuries in a 'natural system' through the so-called law of three generations. Assigning each generation a duration of thirty years and assuming an immediate connection between each generation and the previous and subsequent ones, the century was transformed into a specific natural phenomenon. Even if for Lorenz this triadic connection could transcend the numerical confines of a single century, the fact remains that a historiographical convention was unknowingly projected onto a biological reality and thus transformed into a natural rhythm (Lorenz, pp. 217–311).

In a letter from his youth, Ranke confesses that from the outset he wanted to find 'in the coherent context of grand history (*in dem Zusammenhang der grossen Geschichte*)' what he calls *die Mär*, the 'saga' (or the true novella or 'fable', if we account for the etymological connection between *Märchen* and *Mär*) of world history: 'To find the saga of world history (*die Mär der Weltgeschichte auszufinden*), that process of events (*Begebenheiten*) and the development of our species, which must be considered as its authentic content, its centre and its essence; to grasp and hold fast all the actions and passions of that wild and violent, good and peaceful, contaminated and pure creature that we ourselves are' (Ranke, p. 2). It is significant that precisely for the historian who rejected the abstract categorizations of the philosophy of history, historiographical practice nevertheless leads to 'fable'. In the same way, Toynbee repeatedly emphasizes that history, in the final analysis, can only be constructed in mythical form. Aeonic categories, whether epochal or otherwise, necessarily insinuate themselves into the historian's gaze to make narration possible – and without a narrative element, historical writing is impossible.

12. The fact that the chronology that constitutes the necessary condition of their work has been determined according to criteria that have nothing scientific about them, by obscure monks whose names we scarcely know, does not seem to affect the imperturbable epistemological unconscious of modern historians. This rests on the fact that Christian chronology has been separated from its religious referents – for example, from the birth of Christ as a decisive event in the history of salvation – to become a reference of pure convention. Against this reckless justification, it should be remembered that, as is often the case in such situations, the process of the secularization of Christian chronology did not in any way prevent the historical practice of moderns from inheriting from the chronographies of Julius Africanus and Dionysius Exiguus, and then from the secular calculation of Flacius Illyricus, a series of conceptual implications that are completely unknown to the ancient world, foremost among them the very representation of 'historical' time as a unified whole virtually knowable in its integrity. It was Christianity that constructed the *historikon* that we know as the possible object of historical investigation. This 'historical' time is structured chronologically as a linear whole, whose continuity and meaning are a function of its constitutive finitude, in that it has a beginning and an end. As has been observed, when the numerical element enters historical science, it is always determined qualitatively by the way the beginning of the calculation is fixed. The formation of the very concept of historical time is inseparable from this qualitative relation to a beginning (Heidegger 1916, p. 231). If historical time, as happened in modernity, is instead separated from its

theological context, it necessarily generates contradictions and aporias, against which historical knowledge never ceases to clash.

It is even more evident that the Church's closure of the eschatological window and the secularization of the history of salvation into an infinite linear process betray the genuine messianic exigency that the theological paradigm still contained. Schiller's dictum according to which *die Welgeschichte ist das Weltgericht* [world history is world judgement] can be read, in fact, as a flattening of the two times into the single progress of world history, from which every properly eschatological instant disappears. But it can also be interpreted by seeing in operation in every historical event the instant of a *krisis*, a decisive judgement. It is in this sense that Karl Barth was able to write in his *Römerbrief* that 'the so-called history of salvation is nothing but the continuous crisis of each history, not a history in or alongside history' (Barth 1919, p. 9) and, pushing Ranke's thesis to the extreme, affirms that 'because of its immediacy to God, all history is even ahistorical' (Barth 1958, p. 9). The *eschaton* is not, in this way, the chronological end of historical time, but the irruption of eternity into every moment of history. It therefore makes no sense to speak of a 'Christian history' or 'Christian civilizations': 'Christianity does not produce civilizations, it saves them' (Marrou 1978, p. 359). As we read in another classic of twentieth-century radical eschatology significantly entitled *The Last Things*: 'Each time immediately opens itself to judgement, to its ultimate completion. Every time is, in this sense, the last' (Althaus, p. 174).

13. It is not surprising, from this perspective, that the removal of eschatology is betrayed by the unconscious reappearance in our time of secularized apocalyptic concepts. The final judgement, which has been eliminated in the linear time of history, thus re-emerges forcefully in the concept of 'crisis', which becomes an inseparable

part of the historical-political vocabulary of modernity. Koselleck has shown how this term, originally medical (the 'crisis' in which the doctor must determine whether the patient will die or survive) and theological (the judgement of Christ – *krisis* – on the last day), has gradually spread since the eighteenth century not only in historiography, but also in politics, economics, science and philosophy. If already Leibniz could write that the Europe of his time was 'dans une crise où elle n'a jamais été depuis l'Empire de Charlemagne' (Koselleck, p. 206), in Burkhardt and Marx, crisis designates a phenomenon that recurs periodically in the course of historical processes and, at the same time, the final threshold at which these processes reach their definitive resolution. It is perfectly consistent with these premises that crisis has now ceased to designate a decisive moment and has become a permanent state in every sphere, which must be governed in order to derive the greatest possible profit from it and whose outcome is incessantly delayed. The secularization of the theological model produces a kind of blank eschatology, an apocalypse without redemption or end.

14. The fundamental and non-accessory importance of chronology for modern historiography is manifested in the fact that when we go back in time to a beginning that predates the biblical six days, the chronological grid necessarily loosens and we move to another order of time and research, that of prehistory. Where it is not possible to calculate in years and centuries, history ceases to exist and gives way to something that is not simply a more antique history, but, as every serious historian knows, a reality that is substantially different

from history. This limit is usually equated with the absence of written documents. In reality, it is a problem that every historical investigation must necessarily face whenever it approaches its *arche tes historias*, that is, not only the beginning of chronology, but also the point of origin of the phenomenon it is investigating and, therefore, necessarily its prehistory. History, based on chronology, must have a beginning, but the closer it gets to it, the more it must deal with a prehistoric dimension. When Christian chronography becomes secularized, the beginning can no longer be dated historically, but this does not mean that it loses its necessity. The problem of the chronological and conceptual limit between history and prehistory therefore remains – even if there is a tendency to remove it – the fundamental epistemological problem of historiography.

Since it is based on the isolation and separation of a chronology and a historical time relative to its origin, historiographical investigation must necessarily interpose between itself and the origin an interval in which that chronology remains in some way suspended. Thus, Christian ecclesiastical tradition places between itself and the words of Jesus the prehistoric age of the apostles, which has transmitted those words to ecclesiastical tradition proper, which codified them in canon. In an analogous way, philology places between itself and the original on which the archetype is based, beyond which ecdotic investigation must suspend its criteria. And it is no coincidence that, at the beginning of *The Phenomenology of Spirit*, Hegel places an unwritten sensible truth, whose transcription transforms that truth into a 'history' (*Geschichte*). Historical writing, like all writing, presupposes a non-writing that it claims to transcribe and transmit.

15. The identification, in all historical research, of a fringe or heterogeneous layer, which is not only

located in a chronological position of origin, but also as a qualitative otherness, is due to Franz Overbeck. Overbeck calls *Urgeschichte*, prehistory – or original history – this dimension that all historical research must necessarily confront when approaching the origin understood as the point of emergence (*Entstehung*) of a phenomenon: 'Only by starting from the essential difference between prehistory and history can we explain why prehistory enjoys such special consideration. Prehistory is, in fact, a more relevant and decisive history than any other, and this is in an absolute sense, not only in the history of the Church. The history of the point of origin (*Entstehungsgeschichte*) is, in the history of every living being and, in general, in life, incomparable' (Overbeck, p. 53).

As we trace back the sources and the tradition that have been transmitted to them, the researchers approach the point of origin of the phenomenon, which is divided into *Urgeschichte* and *Geschichte*, prehistory and history, which are connected but not homogeneous, and require different methodologies and precautions. Prehistory does not simply coincide with what is chronologically oldest: 'The fundamental character of prehistory is that it is the history of origins (*Entstehungsgeschichte*) and not, as its name might suggest, that it is ancient (*uralt*). Indeed it can be very young, and the fact of being young or old is not in any case a quality that constitutes it in any original way. This quality is as little perceptible in it as a relationship to time belongs to history in general. Rather, the relationship to time that is proper to it is attributed to it only by the subjectivity of the observer. Like history in general, prehistory is not tied to a particular place in time' (ibid., p. 57).

Seizing a phenomenon at its point of origin means not pushing it back into a remote past, but grasping it in its absolute presence, breaking the chain of tradition that has transmitted it to us. The historian traces documentary sources back to the point where they must necessarily stop at the threshold of the ontological 'source'. Prehistory is, in this sense, always contemporary with history; like the origin according to Benjamin, it acts as a vortex in the flux of historical becoming. In any case, it is essential that historical research that does not measure itself against the prehistory of its object necessarily fails to achieve its aim.

16. In Thesis 17a of *On the Concept of History*, against a historical practice that proceeds through the mere addition of facts, Benjamin lays a claim on a 'constructive principle' for history. A true historian is someone who is able to arrest the empty and homogeneous process of linear history in order to construct its object as a 'constellation' or a 'monad'. 'Thought does not only involve the motion of ideas but also their arrest. When thought suddenly stops in a constellation charged with tension, it imparts a shock to it, causing it to crystallize into a monad. The historical materialist approaches a historical object only and exclusively where it presents itself to him as a monad'. In the methodological notes of the *Passagenwerk*, he clarifies what is meant by monad. Perceiving the monadological structure of the historical object does not only mean making it 'jump out of the continuum of history' (N10,3): it also means perceiving it dialectically and continually split into prehistory and post-history: 'the pre- and post-history (*Vor- und Nach-Geschichte*) of historical fact appear in it thanks to its

dialectical exposition. And again: every historical fact exposited dialectically becomes polarized and a field of forces in which the confrontation (*Auseinandersetzung*) between its pre- and post-history takes place. It becomes so because actuality acts within it. For this reason, the historical fact is polarized according to its pre-and post-history again and again in never the same way' (N7a,1).

We might consider the particular structure the historical object acquires from this perspective. It is no longer an event isolated at a certain point in chronology, but is always a monadic constellation of past and present, prehistory and post-history. As another note points out, 'for the materialist historian, every era he deals with is only prehistory of the era to which he himself belongs. And precisely for this reason, for him there is no appearance of repetition in history, since the moments in the course of history that are most important to him, through their index as "prehistory", become moments of the present itself and change their character according to their catastrophic or triumphal result' (N9a,8).

According to Benjamin, the point of origin of a phenomenon (Overbeck's prehistory) is always situated in the present, and the ability of the historian consists in being able to grasp its prehistoric index each time through a series of divisions and articulations 'until the whole past is brought into the present in a historical apocatastasis' (N1a,3). This means that, according to a radicalization of the messianic paradigm, the *eschaton* coincides here with the present: just as the coming of the messiah divides time irrevocably into a before and an after, so, under the gaze of the historian aware of the theological structure of his object, every single event, insofar as it can be the 'small gate through which the messiah enters', arrests the homogeneous course of events and crystallizes into a monad. 'If every epoch is immediate with respect to God', Benjamin writes, quoting Ranke, 'it is insofar as it is the messianic time of a past epoch' (Benjamin, I.3, p. 1174). As a note in the theses states, 'history is an object of a construction whose place is not homogeneous and empty time, but one filled with the "now" (*Jetzt*)'. And the 'now' is what breaks the continuum of chronological time.

If history has a theological signature, it must not be removed as happens in secularization, but its structure, which we have called 'eschatological difference', must be shown. This is what Benjamin does in his first thesis, revealing that the puppet, 'philosophy of history', is in fact animated by theology. The term 'eschatological difference' refers here to the fact that historical time involves a fundamental asymmetry between a messianic-eschatological moment, which coincides with the present, and the remainder of time. This *eschaton*, which does not simply mean the end of time but a heterogeneity that is constitutively immanent in it, is the passage through which the aeon communicates with chronological time.

Every conception of modern history bears this theological signature and therefore always implies a double structure. When Croce enunciates the principle that all history is contemporary history, because it cannot be separated from the subject who thinks and knows it here and now, or when Augustine affirms that there is no past and future but only a *praesens de praeteritum* and a *praesens de futuris*, they have something similar in view. In any case, the subject of historical knowledge, which is situated in the present, always has to deal with the dual structure of the Christian *historikon*.

17. The concept of the 'historical *a priori*' which defines Foucauldian archaeology also has to do with this heterogeneity immanent to historical time. The term derives

from Husserl's text *On the Origins of Geometry*, which Derrida published in French translation in 1962. Here Husserl, criticizing the claim of historicism, attempts to formulate a conception of historical time that goes beyond the simple history of facts (*Tatsachegeschichte*), in order to define what he calls 'the universal historicity of the correlative mode of being of humanity and the world of culture and the *a priori* structure of this historicity' (Husserl, p. 378).

'Every account of events', he writes, 'remains incomprehensible, because it, by always drawing naïve conclusions directly from the facts, can never address the universal foundation of meaning (*Sinnesboden*) on which those conclusions rest nor has it ever investigated the powerful structural *a priori* that is proper to it. Only the unveiling of the essentially universal structure lies as such in our, or in every, historical past or future present, only in the unveiling of the concrete historical time in which we live, in which our universal humanity lives, in view of its total and general structure, only this unveiling renders history effectively comprehensible and scientific in the true sense of the word. This is the concrete 'historical *a priori*', which encompasses every entity in its becoming and in its historical becoming, or in its essential being as tradition or as something to be transmitted.

The 'historical *a priori*' manifests itself in the present, but, together, constitutes this present as inscribed each time in a universal horizon of meaning that must necessarily be presupposed. The very fact that there is a science that aims to grasp the past as 'what has really taken place' implies the presupposition of this horizon 'that has never been taken into consideration and never thematized': 'every historical problem and every historical demonstration in the current sense presupposes history as a universal horizon of inquiry, not explicitly, but nevertheless as the horizon of certainty which, in every indeterminacy, constitutes the presupposition of every determinability, that is, of every project that aims at the research and fixing of determinate facts' (ibid., p. 382). If Husserl can thereby write that 'in history, the primordial element is our present' (ibid.), it is equally true that the present, in which the historian is situated, must confront, explicitly or implicitly, an *a priori*, which alone gives meaning to his knowledge and renders the series of individual events transmissible and knowable. Here we find that dual structure of time – the eschatological difference – that defines the theological signature of Christian history.

It is significant that it is precisely in the long introduction to his translation of *On the Origin of Geometry* that Derrida elaborates on the concept of *différence* (here still spelled with an *e*), which constitutes the fundamental achievement of his philosophy. According to Derrida, Husserl's conception of the 'historical *a priori*' inscribes in the present, which must constantly confront it, a constitutive deferral that prevents it from coinciding with itself in an absolute presence. 'Le retard est ici l'absolu philosophique, parce que le commencement de la réflexion méthodique ne peut être que la conscience de l'implication d'une autre origine absolue, antérieure et possible en général. Cette altérité de l'origine absolue apparaissant structuralement dans mon "Présent Vivant" et ne pouvant apparaître et être reconnue que dans l'originarité de quelque chose comme mon "Présent Vivant", cela signifie l'authenticité du retard et de la limitation phénomenologique' (Derrida, p. 170). It is precisely what Derrida defines as 'l'impossibilité de se reposer dans la maintenance simple d'un Présent Vivant' that produces 'difference', deferral as a true historical transcendental: 'Transcendantale serait la Différence [. . .]. Transcendentale serait la certitude pure d'une pensée qui, ne pouvant atteindre vers le telos qui s'annonce déjà qu'en avançant vers l'Origine qui indéfiniment se réserve, n'a jamais dû apprendre qu'elle serait toujours à venir. Cette étrange procession d'une *Rückfrage*, tel est le mouvement esquissé dans *L'Origine de la Géometrie*' (ibid., p. 171).

Here we see how the fundamental concept of Derrida's thought is in reality the ontological transposition of a historical-theological concept. Derrida has, in other words, reformulated eschatological difference in terms of ontological difference, in which the decisive moment is already present and yet constitutively refers to another time, which differs from its fulfilment. For this reason, his method could only be articulated as a historical deconstruction of ontology.

18. In *Les mot et les choses*, archaeology, unlike history 'in the traditional sense of the term', is presented as the search for a paradigmatic dimension, a sort of 'historical *a priori*', in which knowledge and understanding find their condition of possibility. Foucault calls this dimension *episteme*: the 'epistemological field in which knowledge, considered outside of any criterion referring to its rational value or its objective forms, founds its positivity and thus manifests a history that is not that of its progressive perfection, but that of its conditions of possibility' (Foucault 1966, p. 13). This is not so much, as Foucault points out, a history of ideas or sciences as part of a research programme that traces, against the current, the history of discursive formations, knowledge and practices, striving to discover 'from what theories and knowledge have been possible; according to what order of space constitutes knowledge; against the background of which "historical *a priori*" and in the context of what positivity ideas were able to emerge, sciences to constitute themselves, experiences to be reflected in

philosophies, rationalities to take shape and then, perhaps, to dissolve and disappear' (ibid.).

Foucault has been criticized for having reproduced, through the 'historical *a priori*', the very duality between prescription and description, regulation and regularity, empirical analysis and archaeological analysis that he had intended to eliminate. While it is true that, in keeping with his characteristic gesture, Foucault never defines his conceptuality *more geometrico*, which therefore sometimes retains ambiguity, it should be remembered that, as *L'Archéologie du savoir* would specify three years later, *episteme* itself is a historical practice, a set of relations that 'in a given epoch can be discovered among the sciences when they are analysed at the level of their discursive regularity' (Foucault, 1969, p. 250). The *a priori*, which conditions the possibility of knowledge, is not a transcendental meta-historical category, but its own history, understood at a particular level. In this sense, archaeology represents, for Foucault, an immanent attempt to come to terms with the aporias of historical knowledge rather than a hierarchically superordinate dimension.

At this point we can clarify the concept of 'historical *a priori*', or, at least, think with less ambiguity the *arché* at stake in historical knowledge. If we call archaeology the practice that seeks to come to terms with the theological aporias of history, then the *arché* it seeks to attain cannot be an origin that occurred at a certain moment in chronology and that once and for all gives meaning to human events. History does not exist because a certain event occurred (the expulsion from paradise, the founding of Rome, the birth of Christ, Muhammad's migration to Medina, the French

Revolution, etc.) that gave human events an indelible historical character. The *arché* in question is not a meta-historical structure or an event that occurred once and for all in chronology; it is, on the contrary, something that never ceases to happen, an event that we cannot precisely situate in chronology and that we must think of as still taking place.

Anthropogenesis is, in this sense, the paradigm of every possible 'historical *a priori*'. Man did not become human *at a certain point* once and for all: rather, he never ceases to become human and to remain inhuman. Anthropogenesis is, therefore, an event that we must necessarily consider to have taken place and, simultaneously, to be equally necessary and contingently ongoing in as much as man is not human once and for all, but *can* be human and, therefore, can not. *History itself is this contingent and, simultaneously, necessary event in which the humanity and inhumanity of man are at stake.* An archaeology will be that knowledge which is maintained each time in relation to anthropogenesis as its own inescapable 'historical *a priori*'. Archaeology thus questions and transforms the experience of chronological time, not because it abolishes or erases it, but because it suspends its efficaciousness. *Chronology is the historical aeon already in the process of being accomplished.* If the decisive event is always ongoing, then history cannot be knowledge of what actually was: it will rather look like memory, of which Benjamin says that, in it, what is accomplished becomes unaccomplished once more and what is unaccomplished becomes accomplished. Insofar as it remains related to anthropogenesis, history is never fulfilled once and for all: rather, its end is, so to speak, always taking place and what has been and what has not been are, in the present instant, equally possible.

In a recent book, Quentin Meillassoux has held in question the necessary correlation between the mind and the world, showing that the human mind can think, as in the natural sciences, about what preceded the appearance of the human mind on earth. Meillassoux calls these events, which are known to predate human history, ancestral. Reflection on ancestry can be usefully related to the problem of *arché* and the 'historical *a priori*'. If it is possible to think of events that precede history and consciousness, it is because anthropogenesis, the production of the human mind, is always ongoing, never fulfilled once and for all. There is here a kind of historical-anthropological Averroism: human thought, insofar as it can be and not be, can think its not yet being. The laws established by the natural sciences are contingent and, simultaneously, necessary; contingent and, simultaneously, necessary is first and foremost thought itself, insofar as it is always in the act of giving itself and not giving itself, of already thinking and not yet thinking.

It is from this perspective that the Heideggerian thesis that being reveals and determines itself in historical epochs should be reinterpreted. It is possible to conceive of a 'history of being' in a non-metaphysical and non-theological way only if the giving of being as the 'historical *a priori*' of philosophy coincides with anthropogenesis, which is conceived as an event that is still taking place. Historical epochs will then correspond not to messages from a meta-historical principle, but to the different ways humanity maintains its relation to the anthropogenetic event of which it is always contemporary, with its becoming more or less human – or, in other words, with the articulation of anthropogenesis in time and with the awareness and memory that individuals and generations have of it. For this reason, since the decisive event is always taking place, neither progress nor regress are really possible.

19. In his *Theological-Political Fragment*, Benjamin forcefully affirms the heterogeneity between the messianic and the sphere of profane time: 'nothing historical', he writes, 'can refer to the messianic of its own accord'. It is important not to overlook all the implications of this clear theorem. Messianic concepts – which Benjamin correctly exemplifies with that of the Kingdom – have 'no political meaning, but only religious' and can therefore never be set as goals of political action, of which they represent the radical crisis: 'for this reason, the Kingdom of God is not the *telos* of the historical dynamic: it cannot be set as a goal. From a historical point of view, it is not a goal (*Ziel*), but an end (*Ende*)'. The messianic is, at every moment, the end and the annihilation of the entire sphere of profane time, and no politics can claim to be built upon it. Hence the significance of the thesis that concludes the fragment, according to which the method of world politics 'must be called nihilism'.

If we recall that, in Thesis 17a in *On the Concept of History*, Benjamin writes that 'in the idea of a classless society, Marx secularized the idea of messianic time', then it is possible that the concept of revolution, so present in the theses, should also be considered, like that of the Kingdom, a messianic concept. The error of social democracy, which has transformed the messianic into an infinite task, but also that of the entire Marxist tradition, would then consist, from the perspective of the fragment, in having transformed what is set as a *goal* what can only be an *end*, in having sought to historically achieve what can only act in history by remaining unattainable. For this reason, only those classes are revolutionary, in the theses, which by introducing an absolutely heterogeneous temporality, are capable of 'breaking the continuum of history' and producing a 'messianic arrest of happening'. And precisely decisive are those concepts – Kingdom, revolution, anarchy – which, inasmuch as they can never be set as a goal, act, so to speak, only nihilistically on world politics. The error of modern politics is to have wanted to set as the goal of human historical progress that which, being radically heterogeneous to it, can only mark its annihilation and arrest *here and now*. In removing its own constitutive eschatological tradition, it has condemned itself to a failure from which there is no escape.

20. The very concept of archaeology needs to be further clarified from this perspective. Reiner Schürmann, in his anarchic interpretation of Heidegger, distinguishes between two concepts of origin: the first, which he calls 'original', designates the beginning that determines and initiates a certain historical development, and a second, which he calls 'originary', denotes the pure and ahistorical coming into presence, the 'emergence that comes into presence at the very moment it withdraws into itself'. The original, as a beginning, designates the establishment of a historical era, which, according to Schürmann, coincides with the object of Foucauldian archaeology; the originary, on the other hand, designates the ahistorical arising into presence. In assigning to thought the task of retracing the path from the original to the originary, from the investigation of the historical modalities of presence to the ahistorical coming to presence itself, Schürmann nevertheless remains trapped in the aporias of origin he had sought to circumvent.

A truly anarchic archaeology cannot maintain a concept of origin, even if it is relegated to a time before or beyond any historical epoch. The decisive significance of archaeology can only be truly understood if it is specified that the *arché* or point of emergence that it seeks does not coincide with the origin, but is located in the gap between the origin and the historical tradition of knowledge. The only point of emergence that archaeology can reach is located, to make use of Schürmann's terminology, between the original and the originary, in the interval that separates the patient and inescapable investigation of historiographical knowledge from the origin that it intends to draw out and circumscribe. If, to use Overbeck's terminology, we call this gap 'prehistory', then the relation between history and prehistory, between the tradition of knowledge and the prehistoric interstice that separates it from the *arché*, will be essential in any archaeological investigation.

The practice of philological investigation has always sought to define the space which separates it from the origin and to establish itself productively in it. Since in classical philology the original is necessarily missing, Lachmann's method for editing texts assumes a codex that does not actually exist, called the archetype, which can be traced back by comparing the errors contained in the existing codices. In other words, it is assumed that between the original and the attested codices there exists a lost manuscript, which may even be much later than the autograph, from which the known manuscripts derive through a process that is formalized in a sort of genealogical tree. The archetype, however, does not exist anywhere and, on closer inspection, expresses nothing more than the gap that separates the historically attested codices from the original. When philologists, as often happens, claim to materialize the archetype in all its details (including the form of writing), they unwittingly transform prehistory into history and forget that the archetype expresses nothing more than the relation that unites and, at the same time, separates the existing manuscripts and the absent original.

In psychoanalysis, the mechanism that allows us to trace a series of existing phenomena – pathological symptoms, such as the *lapsus* – back to a repressed event, which functions in relation to them, is similar to the archetype relative to historically attested codes. Freud supposes, that is, the existence of an unknown event, the memory of which, due to its traumatic nature, has been repressed into the unconscious and, while remaining latent, produces neurotic symptoms and can, therefore, explain them. In *Moses and Monotheism*, Freud seeks to extend the scheme of repression from the individual level to that of the 'tradition of the psychic life of a people'. After the traumatic imposition of the law by Moses, the Mosaic religion entered a phase of latency, only to reappear later in the form of a Jewish monotheism with which we are familiar. Freud thus establishes a parallel between the historical tradition of Judaism and the contents repressed in the unconscious.

Cathy Caruth suggested, developing Freud's theories, that a form of latency and repression is constitutive of historical experience and that it is precisely and only through its oblivion that the historical event is in some way preserved. Historical experience is, in other words, always traumatic in itself and can only be experienced through its repression. 'The historical power of trauma', writes Caruth, 'lies not so much in the fact that the traumatic experience resurfaces and is repeated after its oblivion, but in the fact that only though its inherent oblivion can it be experienced [. . .]. That history is the history of trauma means that it is meaningful only to the extent that it is not fully perceived as it occurs, or, in other words, that history can only be understood in the very inaccessibility of its occurrence' (Caruth, pp. 17–18).

We can now better understand how the point of origin that archaeology aims at cannot coincide with an origin located at a certain point in historical chronology, but rather lies in the gap between historical tradition and origin. Every present is, so to speak, traumatic; that is, it contains a part of the unlived and forgotten, which cannot be hypostasized in an origin rejected in the past, but rather expresses a split inherent in historical experience itself. For humans, as animals endowed with language and consciousness, the gap between historical knowledge and the point of origin cannot be eliminated and constitutes historical experience as an errancy, exposing it to those deficiencies and gaps exemplified in classical philology by the errors of copyists and in psychoanalysis by neurotic slips of the tongue.

It should now be even clearer why history is constitutively split into *res gestae* and *historia rerum gestarum*. Between these two sides of historical experience there is an unavoidable disconnect, and only if we become aware of this and resolutely position ourselves within it will our historical investigations eventually bear fruit. And it is in this unavoidable gap that the root of that historical possibility lies, the discovery and definition of which are an indispensable part of archaeological research. Only if we manage to place our investigations in the prehistoric gap between knowledge and origin will we be able to know not only or not so much the actuality of the *res gestae*, but also or rather what made them possible and still preserves their possibility. The point of emergence thus understood is an event always taking place, an internal source within the flux of events which, as such, never ceases to occur, and not an origin rejected at the beginning of a chronology. Anthropogenesis, which is the paradigm of origin and its inaccessibility, remains possible at every moment in human history.

2
Recapitulation and Salvation

1. The term 'recapitulation', *anakephalaiosis* and the verb *anakephalaiousthai*, to recapitulate, originally belongs to the vocabulary of ancient rhetoric. 'It is the work of rhetoric', reads a fragment by Aristotle, 'to make introductions to arouse benevolence, to narrate to make people believe, to discuss to demonstrate, to recapitulate to make people remember (*anakephalaiosasthai pros anamnesin*)'. And Quintilian, in his *Institutes of Oratory*, specifies that 'the repetition and gathering of things (*rerum repetitio et congregatio*), which the Greeks call *anakephalaiosis* and some Latins *enumeration*, enumeration, refresh the memory of judges and simultaneously place the whole case before their eyes' (VI, 1, 1). The recapitulation is, that is, a compendium for mnemonic purposes of all the arguments extensively presented in the course of a peroration. *Kaphalaion* designates both the head (or leader) and the main or 'capital' point of the speech or question (*en kephalaioi eipein* therefore means 'to speak in sum, to summarize)'.

In a passage from his Letter to the Ephesians, Paul uses this rhetorical term to express a decisive point of his messianic doctrine. After expounding the divine plan of redemption, he defines it in this way: 'for the economy of the fullness of time, all things are recapitulated in Christ (*eis oikonomian tou pleromatos ton kairon anakephalaiosasthai ta panta en Christoi*), both those in heaven and those on earth' (1:10). This means that in messianic time – inasmuch as it concerns the fullness or fulfilment (*pleroma*) of times – a recapitulation takes place, a sort of summary of all things in Christ, that is, of everything that has happened from creation to the messianic 'hour'. It is no coincidence that the two terms 'recapitulation' and '*pleroma*' are found side by side, as is also the case in the Letter to the Romans, 13:9–11, where Paul writes that, with the coming of the Messiah, every commandment 'is summed up (*anakephalaioutai*) in this phrase: you shall love your neighbour as yourself', adding immediately after that 'love is the *pleroma*, the fulfilment of the law'.

2. It is said that dying people see their entire existence flash before their eyes in an instant, in a dizzying, panoramic abridgement. Bergson, in his analysis of memory, refers to the case of drowned or hanged people who were about to die of suffocation and, once they had returned to life, declared that they had 'seen in a short time all the forgotten events of their lives in the smallest details and in the same order in which they occurred' (Bergson 1939, p. 172). The testimonies emphasize the instantaneous and simultaneous nature of this vision. De Quincey, recounting the story of a relative of his who fell into a river as a child, writes that 'she saw in a single

instant her whole life in the smallest incidents, arranged simultaneously before her as in a mirror'. 'At death', reports another witness, 'the whole of life is summed up in an indivisible instant, and at that moment, everything that came after becomes instantaneous' (Ballanche, p. 134). The impression of simultaneity is so strong that those who have experienced it have compared it to an experience of divine eternity: 'those who are about to die have in their final moment an intense and simultaneous vision of the totality of events that have occurred in their existence. I know this from experience. To express it one would need to modify Plato's famous formula and say that in this case time becomes the immutable image of immutable eternity. Thus, from the image I can trace back to reality and conceive of God's eternity. Try to imagine how I continue this accidental state, eliminating the succession and flight of time: everything that was elusive and seemed ungraspable becomes fixed for a moment, the vertigo ceases and the mind, without disturbance or hesitation and without contradicting itself, can grasp the eternal present of pure duration' (Poulet, p. 148).

Coming back a few years later to reflect on the relation between memory and the panoramic vision of the dying, Bergson compares the latter to the perception of a melody which, when listened to, 'appears to us from beginning to end as an eternal present'. 'In exceptional cases', he adds, 'attention suspends the interest he felt for life: immediately, as if by a spell, the past then becomes present again. In those who suddenly see the threat of sudden death looming before them, in the mountaineer who slips into a precipice, in those who are drowning or hanging themselves, there seems to be an abrupt conversion of attention, something like a change in the orientation of consciousness' (ibid., p. 177).

3. The undoubtedly religious tone of these testimonies suggests that the panoramic vision of the dying presents more than an analogy with the messianic recapitulation. As with the dying, in recapitulation the events of the past are torn from linear profane time and placed in connection with the messianic *Kairos*. That, in this sense, in it the times and the law come to fulfilment means that *anakephalaiosis* is nothing more than the other side of the typological relation which, according to Paul, messianic time establishes between the past and the present. Invoking, in the First Letter to the Corinthians, a series of episodes from the history of Israel, Paul stated that 'these things that took place for the Jews as figures of us (*hos typoi emon*)' and 'happened figuratively (*typikos*) and were written for our instruction, for us, in whom the ends of the times stand faced with each other' (1 Cor. 10:1–11). This 'figurative' conception (Jerome will translate *typoi* in 1 Cor. 10:6 with *in figura*) of human history became the foundation of a general theory of allegorical interpretation in the Christian middle ages. Through the concept of *typos*, however, Paul establishes something more than a symbolic relation between every event of the past and *ho nyn kairos,* messianic time. Thus, in Rom. 5:14, Adam, through whom sin entered the world, becomes *typos tou mellontos*, 'figure of the one who is to come', that is, the messiah, who, as second Adam, will redeem humanity from the sin committed by the first. Every moment of the present is in a figurative relation with an event of the past, which finds its true meaning and fulfilment in it.

What is decisive here is that the fullness of time is understood as the relation of each moment with the messiah, and not, according to the paradigm that Hegel will leave as a legacy to Marx and modernity, as the final result of a process. As in Ranke's historiographical theorem, every moment, every *kairos*, is *unmittelbar zu Gott*, in immediate relation to God. Every historical moment is the 'hour' of the messiah, and the messianic is not the chronological end of time, but the present as a need for fulfilment and salvation. If, according to Ranke's image, every generation is equidistant from God, then, as a contemporary theologian has suggested, not only every epoch, but also every personal existence is immediately related to the messiah: 'For every civilization and every human generation, as for every living man, it must be recognized that its last and only day [. . .] is the Last Day [. . .]. All time participates in, from this perspective, an eschatological quality' (Marrou 1979, p. 107). The typological relation between past event and the present coincides with their being in an immediate relation to God and the recapitulation of what has been restores this immediacy. Recapitulating means, for the individual as well as the community, fulfilling time, reintegrating and saving that which has been lived – or missed – in the fullness of the present moment.

4. Hence its proximity to another category of patristic theology: apocatastasis. The term, which was used in law to indicate the restitution of patrimonial goods and in medicine for the restoration of an injured limb, originally belongs to the vocabulary of astronomy, where it designates the return of the stars to their original position. Origen uses it several times to name a concept that

is particularly important to him: the final restitution of all beings to their original condition in God. This ultimate apocatastasis of all things seemed so indispensable to him that he did not hesitate to risk condemnation as a heretic by asserting that at the end of time even Satan and the fallen angels would be restored to their original perfection. In Jerome's words of reproach, who nevertheless admired him unreservedly, Origen dared to maintain that 'in the future restoration of all things, not only will all sinners be absolved, but even the devil himself with his angels will be released from punishment, so that the restoration of all things may be understood in a coherent manner' (Ramelli, p. 18).

Although Origen expresses himself cautiously on this subject, he knows perfectly well that apocatastasis can only refer to all creatures without any possible exceptions. If all creatures will be restored to their original condition in God, it is because they come from God and have never ceased to be in him. It is not as a devil or rebellious angel that Satan will be saved, but as a creature of God, and 'every soul dwells always in the Logos, always in wisdom, always in God' (*De Princ.*, II, 6.6). For in the end, when everything is consummated, every soul will return to God: 'The end', reads his commentary on John, 'comes in the so-called apocatastasis, in which no one will remain an enemy, if it is true, as it is written (1 Cor. 15:24–26) that "he will reign until he has placed all his enemies under his feet" and the last enemy, death, will be rendered inoperative' (Origen, p. 107).

It is no coincidence that Benjamin, who had transformed theological redemption into a historical category, was fascinated with Origen's theories. In his essay on Leskov he recalls 'Origen's theses rejected by the

Roman church' on the entry of all souls into paradise. Influenced, like the entire Orthodox tradition, by the Alexandrian theologian, Leskov interpreted resurrection as liberation from an incantation. This incantation is history as we know it. In a note in the *Passagenwerk* on historical method (N1a,3), Benjamin again quotes Origen without naming him, writing that the entire past must be 'placed in the present in a sort of historical apocatastasis'. The restoration of all things to their origin implies that they must first be introduced into the eschatological present, where recapitulation takes place. Recapitulation – the abbreviated summary – is the form in which creatures are brought back to God. *Anakephalaiosis* and apocatastasis are inseparable.

5. In the idea of eternal return, Nietzsche also sought something like apocatastasis. It is with this term that a Christian source defines, in fact, the Stoic doctrine of universal palingenesis, which inspired the philosopher's supreme thought: 'The Stoics claim that the planets will return (*apokathistamenous*) to the same constellation [. . .]. Apocatastasis, universal restitution, does not occur only once, but many times and the same things will return infinitely' (Ramelli, p. 7).

Nietzsche, however, conceives his apocatastasis as an eternal return of the same in the smallest, even capricious, details: 'And this slow spider climbing in the moonlight, and this same moonlight, and you and I under the door whispering together about eternal things, must we not all have been before? And must we not return and run on the other road before us, on this long, gruesome road, must we not return eternally?' (Nietzsche, p. 192). But salvation cannot simply be the repetition of the same. Nietzsche's mistake is to have separated apocatastasis and recapitulation, producing a sort of parody of salvation.

Origen, for his part, was careful to introduce a distinction between that which has been and what is saved. He criticizes the doctrine of the eternal return because it sacrifices the very freedom it should save: 'It is clear that only out of necessity will Socrates always return to devote himself to philosophy, he will always be accused of corrupting the youth by introducing new gods, and Anytus and Meletus will always be his accusers, and the Areopagus will condemn him to death [. . .]. If we accept this idea, I do not understand how our freedom can be saved and rewards and punishments justified' (Ramelli, p. 9). Intervening in the dispute that divided the Fathers on the state of the body at the moment of resurrection (will it be identical to the one decrepit and disfigured by death, or instead in the perfection of youth?), he specifies that what is resurrected is not the exact same body, but its *eidos*, its idea or figure. The *eidos* is the form in which what has been is recapitulated and abbreviated in order to be restored to eternity. And it is only thanks to this precious miniature that apocatastasis ceases to be the nightmare [*incubo*] of an eternal return of infinite, meticulous, insignificant details, with which Nietzsche never managed to come to terms.

6. The connection between apocatastasis, recapitulation and figure is evident in the theologian who developed a true theory of *anakephalaiosis*, Irenaeus of Lyons. He knew that salvation through Christ is conceivable only if the three concepts are held together. The incarnation, in fact, acquires its full reality, distinct from the eternal pre-existence of the messiah that was already familiar to Judaism, only because, by becoming man, Christ recapitulated in himself the whole history of humanity. If it is certain, he writes, that the Son already existed with the Father, 'when he became incarnate and became man, he recapitulated in himself the whole long history of humanity, giving us complete salvation, so that what we had lost in Adam, we might regain in Jesus' (*Adversus haereses*, III, 18.1). Redemption is true and effective and can 'kill sin' because Christ's generation recapitulated that of Adam: 'Just as the substance of Adam, the first man formed, was taken from simple and still virgin earth [. . .] taking mud from the earth, so it was fitting that the Word of God should receive a generation that recapitulated that of Adam, he who, being born of Mary, still a virgin girl, was to recapitulate Adam in himself' (III, 21.10). The ultimate meaning of the incarnation is, therefore, recapitulation: 'This is why the Lord is called the Son of Man, because he recapitulates in himself the first man: just as through a man who was conquered death entered our race, so through the work of another man, we obtain victory' (IV, 21.1). It is clear that, for Irenaeus, recapitulation and typology coincide perfectly. The figurative relation between the past and present is not simply an allegory. By recapitulating Adam in himself, Christ fulfils what was *typos* and figure. What is at stake is not a metaphor or a shadow, but salvation, restitution and the preservation of the past. In the figure – and only in this – what has been is restored to its original condition in God.

7. The recapitulative and typological identity forces us to rethink what we are accustomed to calling

prefiguration and allegory. The figural relation is not limited to adding a new meaning to something – an event in the past – which refers it to something other than itself – the present. Rather, it constitutes the present as a recapitulation of the past, but this abridged summary coincides, in the past event, with its being a *typos* and figure of the future. Only insofar as the gaze of the present moment recapitulates the past event in a drastic glance does it become a figure of the present, The figure does not precede that of which it is a figure, but coincides with its being recapitulated and transfigured; and, conversely, recapitulation is nothing more than the fulfilment of the figural character of the past. In the words of Eriugena, Christ indissolubly unites in himself what seems separate, 'paradise and the globe, heaven and earth, the intelligible and the sensible, for, as we have both body and senses, soul and intellect, he, uniting each single thing with its extreme counterpart, has divinely recapitulated all things in himself' (Eriugena, *De divisione naturae*, V). Hence the enigmatic and even disturbing aspect of the allegories and emblems that from Alciato's *Emblemata* to the late seventeenth-century editions of Cesare Ripa's *Iconologia*, have so captivated humanists, painters and poets. If the objects and the images represented are unrecognizable, it is because they have been forcibly ripped from their context, recapitulated and transported to another place and time. Recapitulation and typology are, in other words, the two tensions that transform chronological time into messianic time, simple prefiguration into salvation. Hence, too, the difference between voluntary memory and involuntary recollection, on which both Bergson and Proust have meditated so insistently. What appears in the recollection of memory is not the same image that memory preserved in its archives: what was definitely and irrevocably accomplished in it now becomes presentiment and figure and what was unfulfilled in it now finds its fulfilment and can thus be restored to its original condition in God.

8. What is meant by being saved, to be brought back to God? Being in God is not a topographical fact; it cannot be the object of factual observation. Rather, in order for human beings to perceive it, it must stake on that particular form which we have so far designated by the term 'recapitulation'. To see something in God means, in Spinoza's words, to see it outside of space and time, *sub quadam aeternitatis specie*. But what form does a thing have when we contemplate it 'in a species of eternity'?

In his review of Julien Green's *Adrienne Mesurat*, Benjamin observes that Green does not describe people, but depicts them vividly as they appear 'at a fateful moment', forever captured in a gesture that defines them: 'Adrienne Mesurat, who stops dusting to look at the family portraits; old Mesurat, who strokes his beard; Madame Legras, who walks away with Adrienne's necklace: each of their gestures would be exactly the same if they were deceased souls who had to relive these moments from beyond the grave' (Benjamin, III, p. 154). It is possible to name 'gesture' the form that everything takes in recapitulation, the abbreviation in which an entire existence contracts at the moment of its return to God. If *typos* is the figure and recapitulation its fulfilment, salvation will result from their coincidence in a gesture. And only the gesture is responsible for that 'species of eternity' through which we contemplate things in God for an instant.

The eternity that is in question here is really only a 'species', an aspect or an appearance. And, yet, this species implies a genuinely ontological problem, which concerns the relation between God and his modes. These – the infinite, singular creatures, living beings, flowers, springs, stars – are not able to be distinguished from God as one thing from another, but *being-in* defines their specific mode of being. God is in all things only to the extent that all things are in God. This absolute reciprocity requires that the two categories with which metaphysics has thought about being be called into question: existence and essence. Neither does God constitute the essence of his modes, nor do they identify his existence. They are, immemorably, eternally in each other and one in the other. In this mutual, forgetful dwelling, they coincide, that is, they fall together.

Being-in is, in this sense, a gesture. The gesture is the figure in which everything appears to us at the point in which we suddenly realize that it is in God and that God is in it.

9. One of the witnesses who recounted the hypermnesic vision of his entire existence at the moment he was about to drown reports that at that very moment he felt something like a sense of peace. 'From the moment all my efforts ceased – due, I suppose, to the suffocation I was experiencing – a feeling of calm, of the most perfect serenity, replaced the turmoil of my previous sensations. It could have been called apathy, but certainly not resignation, because drowning no longer seemed like a bad thing to me' (Poulet, p. 156). In the moment in which

our life is recapitulated and passes before us in the blink of an eye, we somehow detach ourselves from it. And yet, the figures and things appear to us with greater intensity, as we detach them from their spatio-temporal context and bid them farewell. They are safe, but, so to speak, not *for us*.

In any case, one of the essential purposes of recapitulation seems to be precisely that of allowing us to calmly separate ourselves from our past. Precisely for this reason, it is important to detach recapitulation from any exclusive connection with the end of time and death. In the course of our existence, at decisive moments, we often experience recapitulation and feel that only in this way can we continue to live. And yet, the past from which we have thus separated only now acquires its full meaning; only now can we truly remember it and not simply file it away in the archives of memory. Only what, in recapitulation, has been consigned to a gesture and thus detached from our immediate impulses and desires, only what we contemplate in this sense *sub quadam aeternitatis specie*, can now nourish and make us live.

10. What appears to us at this point is not simply the past, the life we have lived. At the very moment when, by handing over what has been in a gesture, it allows us to take leave of it, the recapitulation discloses its true object. Which is not what has been, but what has never been – not what we have experienced, but what has remained unlived in our lives.

Leopardi once wrote that the life we would like to relive is not the one we know, but the one we do not know, that is, the life we have not lived. However, the life we have not lived is secretly contained in the one we have lived. And not as something completely different, an imaginary life we could have lived, which has nothing to do with the one we have lived. What has never been is the figure in which our life appears to us when, taking leave of it, we perceive it in God. As in Caproni's poem, we have never been there, but only return – there where 'everything / remains just as / I left it', there we find the glass we never filled half full. And only at this point are we given something like a new beginning – not as an origin to reclaim, but as the night – anarchic and unlived, and which can only remain so – at the centre of everything we have experienced. Because only what has never been experienced can one day – this day, here and now – be fulfilled.

3
Tradition and Its Source

1. Every attempt to comprehend what 'tradition' means must begin with the awareness that tradition and what it claims to transmit – the source – are and are not the same thing, that the act of *transmission* – the *traditio* – exceeds necessarily its *traditum* in every respect, even as it cannot in any way be separated from it. This means that tradition is constitutively doubled, that it exists in two distinct and articulated forms, and that it is not possible to know a tradition without knowing the modalities of this articulation. Precisely because tradition is distinct from its source and yet inseparable from it, Ignatius of Antioch was able to write that it refers rather to its silence, to what the source has kept silent.

2. In the Christian Church, which at a certain point codified the object of its tradition in a canon, a distinction is usually made between holy Scripture and tradition, the latter term referring to the collection of texts, oral discourses and liturgical practices that the

Church has added to the former throughout its history. The convention is that the canon is based on the revelation given by God to the apostles and that it is this canon that the post-apostolic ecclesiastical tradition preserves, interprets and transmits. The work of the apostles continues in the work of the Church, so that Scripture and tradition have their common foundation in Christ. Even minimal philological caution shows that the distinction between the apostolic revelation and the ecclesial tradition has no basis: as far as we know, it was the Church, in a relatively late period (between the end of the second and end of the fourth centuries), that established the canon we know today. The particular status of this source is, in other words, the work of tradition, which is split into a presupposed canon and its transmission. For this reason, from a historical point of view, particular attention must be paid to the period preceding the formation of the canon, on which documents are, by definition, scarce. Since the source is only a presupposition of tradition, no historical tradition ever goes back to its source, but is necessarily separated from it by a period of time that we can consider, with Overbeck, its prehistory.

3. The situation is similar with respect to the tradition of Judaism. It distinguishes between two *Torahs*, the written and the oral. That this is a fundamental splitting of the tradition, which does not coincide with the fact of writing is evidenced in the fact that even the oral Torah, defined as a 'hedge' around Scripture, can be transcribed, as happened with the Talmud. The establishment of the biblical canon also took place relatively late, towards the end of the first century CE; and here too, the texts

that compose it are traced back to a prehistoric oral tradition, which has its origin on Sinai. 'The Scriptures, the tradition, the decisions of the doctors and what a devout disciple can teach, all this', says the Talmud, 'was given to Moses on Sinai'. The oral Torah was given to Moses together with the written – that is, they are both distinct and inseparable. 'Moses', reads the Mishnah, 'received the Torah on Mount Sinai and transmitted it to Joshua; Joshua transmitted it to the Elders; the Elders transmitted it to the prophets, and the prophets to the men of the Great Synagogue'. The split between *traditum* and *tradition* is, together, both constitutive and unverifiable. What we have is a single tradition, which claims to exist in two distinct and articulated forms.

4. It is assumed that the source – the origin – is distinct from its tradition and, nevertheless, accessible only through it, and that it is inevitably exposed to corruption. As classical philologists teach us, we have no access to the moment when the poet gave form to his poetry: but as soon as he dictates it to a scribe, as soon as the poetry is handed down, it can immediately be betrayed, there is the possibility of error. In the same way, we do not have access to the moment when Jesus utters his words; but as soon as someone – even an apostle – collects and transcribes them, as soon as a tradition begins, the possibility of corruption insinuates itself.

The aporia – in the literal sense of the term: absence of a path – consists here in the fact that tradition and source cannot coincide and that, nevertheless, we have no other access to the source than through tradition. For this reason, those who adhere to a tradition tend, more or less consciously, to privilege it over the source, which is in some way crystallized and neutralized. The canonization of a text coincides in this sense with its ceasing to be a source and with its subordination to tradition, which nevertheless claims to have its foundation therein. The text is accessible only through a transmission that by definition cannot lead to it: this is the vicious circle of every tradition, which can also be expressed by stating that tradition is an entirely historical operation that tends to split itself in two and places its *traditum* outside history.

5. Such is the inescapable historical lesson of philology. As the title of Pasquali's masterpiece suggests, *History of Tradition and Text Criticism*, only a critical understanding of the history of tradition allows us to access the text we intend to read, but this is not – or almost never is – the original, but what we can achieve by tracing back the history of the tradition that has transmitted it to us. In Lachmann's stemma, the archetype to which the philologist traces the variously historically attested manuscripts is not only not the original, but is itself already broken and disfigured, and it is only by comparing the corruptions and errors common to several manuscripts that their archetype could be reconstructed. The corollary of this theorem is that we receive our culture – like our language – through a historical tradition, but this is always already consciously or unconsciously corrupted and altered and needs to be amended and interpreted. This means that the dialectic between source and tradition is the problem *par excellence* – and as such, principally political – of human history, and that any thought which does not account for it will inevitably fail to achieve its purpose.

6. What we see before us today is the separation and almost rupture between tradition and its source, between transmission and what it should transmit. Talmudic tradition distinguishes between Halachah (and Law or truth itself, as a purely prescriptive statement) and Aggadah (that is, the truth in its tradability, the collections of anecdotes that communicate and make the Law comprehensible). The current situation of western culture can be defined by saying that an irreparable rift has developed between Halachah and Aggadah, between the truth to be transmitted and its transmission. There is – or rather, there is supposed to be – a truth, but no possibility of transmission; there are means of transmission, but they transmit nothing. The dispositives and institutions that should pass on the sources have multiplied to excess: yet schools, universities, academies, museums, colleges and libraries have never been so incapable of performing their task. Sources, which can only live if they are made present again and remain in some way alive, are irrevocably relegated to the past, and culture is transformed into an endless heritage of dead artefacts that accumulate in the places assigned for their preservation. Tradition has mortified and killed its *tradendum*; truth and law have become disconnected from life.

7. We must hold in question the very idea that there can be a truth separate from its tradition, a canon distinct from its transmission, a rule divided from its use. Where such a split has occurred through a millennial process, the task of study is to trace the tradition archaeologically back to the point where the break occurred. This point, which we can call the point of

origin, in order to distinguish it from the presupposed origin, is not found in the chronological past, but is located in the gap between tradition and its source, in what Overbeck called prehistory and which occurs each time in the present, at the point where the individual confronts the truth of a text or word. If what is sourced can never acquire a consistency separate from its transmission, the prerequisite for any study – and this is its salutary barbarism – will be the decisive rejection of all categories through which the source assumes a rank and prestige that separates it from its tradability: sacredness, artistic creation, good culture, civilization, doctrine, creation and whatever other exemptions contribute to canonizing it. The scholar will rather forcibly rip the work, text or image with which he or she is dealing from its historically constructed context, not to even further isolate it, but to return them to their source, prehistoric – that is, present – indivisibility, where something like a tradition cannot be distinguished from its *tradendum*.

8. Every tradition proceeds from the past, that is, from the dead, and it is with them that we must therefore in some way make contact. The Greeks called this invocation of the dead *nekyia*, significant examples of which were the eleventh canto of *The Odyssey* and, in Rome, the sixth canto of *The Aeneid*. A sort of *nekyia* occurs in every tradition, if it is not to be simply a more or less decent funeral, as Steinschneider believed. And since in this case we are dealing primarily – though not exclusively – with texts, the problem here is how to make them speak again without spilling the 'black and smoking' blood of sacrificial animals. Those who

approach the texts of the past must accept to offer them their voice, so that only their words speak though them. This means that, in a living tradition, the *origo*, the source of the word, does not belong to the one who utters it, but to others. But, on closer inspection, it does not even belong to the dead person from whom it comes, because, if it is not simply a doxographic repetition of a canon, it is uttered – or written – as if for the first time by the voice – or hand – of the person who receives it. In this sense, the original word is the word that belongs to no one, of which no one can claim to be the author. The origin of the word is, in other words, a complex operation in which two voices affirm and negate each other in a sort of prehistoric non-place.

It is similar to the *origo* in the tradition of Roman public law, which is always elsewhere than the place where it is to be enforced. Thus, the origin of Rome was not in Rome, but in Lavinium, where Aeneas had landed and where *dii penates* and the *sacra primordia* resided; but Lavinium, for what remains, was a perfectly empty place, a pure legal fiction. Analogously, the *origo* of every citizen was not the city in which he was born, but where his first ancestor was born; it was, that is, a 'from', not an 'in', it was in the ablative and never in the locative. And this is precisely the structure of tradition, divided into a 'from' and an 'in', because what ultimately has to be transmitted, the true *tradendum*, is tradition itself: *traditionis traditio*.

9. A clear example of how the split between transmission and the thing to be transmitted is produced is language. We are continually and exclusively dealing with acts of speech and instances of discourse, and yet tradition has so accustomed us to identifying what we do when we speak with the exercise of a language that we forget that something like a language has been constructed through a patient, centuries-long process of interpretation and grammatical canonization of the act of speech. The Saussurean distinction between *langue* and *parole*, which is perfectly familiar to us today, is, in this sense, the archetype of the doubled character of every human tradition. Humans transmit language to each other by speaking, and yet they act as if they were transmitting an entity of reason, consisting of a lexicon and a set of grammatical and syntactical rules, which is called a 'language'. What has been constructed from the discourses that speakers exchange is thereby relegated to the past as the origin that they must presuppose in order to understand each other, as if the word 'tree' combined with other words in a real instance of discourse could only mean something because the lemma 'tree [*albero*]', taken in itself and isolated from any discourse, means 'tree [*albero*]' in the language we call Italian. It is perhaps properly because we have split our experience of language into two incommunicable planes that we can then divide truth from its transmission, *tradendum* from its *tradition*. But, as in language, it is not so much a matter of seeking an arch-grammar that can account for our discourses and conversation, as how to reach, beyond the fracture between language and word – or rather, in their falling together – the living voice in its poetic wellspring [*sorgvità*], so that in every tradition that claims to be founded on a source, we do not need to regress to an origin that is in reality inaccessible: instead, rather, faced with a simple truth that touches us, we must draw, in a sort of relentless *nekyia*, on the prehistoric coincidence of source and tradition that constitutes its unique life.

4
Mundus patet

1. In modern thought the link between man and the world is so close that the very form of human existence has been defined as 'being-in-the-world'. Being-in-the-world, dwelling – as we read in what is considered the masterpiece of twentieth-century philosophy – is not 'a property that being sometimes has and sometimes does not have, and without which it could be as it is, neither more nor less than having it. It is not that man is and, in addition to that, has a relation with the world that is occasional and arbitrary. *Dasein* is not first and foremost an entity without being, which occasionally thinks of taking up a relation with the world. The assumption of a relation with the world is possible only insofar as *Dasein* is what it is only as being-in-the-world' (Heidegger 1927, p. 127). In this sense, 'worldliness' is an 'ontological concept' inseparable from human experience and the adjective 'worldly' 'always means a way of *Dasein* and never a way of being the entity available "in" the world'. It is therefore unsurprising that around

thirty paragraphs of *Being and Time* are devoted to the analysis of this fundamental structure of human existence.

A year later, in *On the Essence of Ground*, Heidegger returns to being-in-the-world and explores its definition in greater depth. Here, world does not mean, in the usual sense, the totality of what exists, but the essential constitution of human existence, which, as such, is always in the act of going beyond every entity and, above all, the entity that it itself is. That man is in-the-world means that he is a being of transcendence, always already caught up in a process of going beyond; and 'that towards which (*woraufhin*) *being* as such transcends, we call world' (Heidegger 1929, p. 641). The term 'world' thus loses its obviousness and designates both the movement of going beyond and that towards which it proceeds. And at this point, Heidegger feels compelled to sketch 'albeit in a necessarily fragmentary way' (ibid., p. 644), a brief history of the concept.

2. Although the lacuna had been announced, the summariness and tendentiousness of this genealogy cannot fail to surprise. Greek thought is represented by only four fragments from the pre-Socratics (Melissus, fr. 7; Parmenides, fr. 2; Anaxagoras, fr. 8; Heraclitus, fr. 89), which, except for the Heraclitian, are not quoted in full. The aim is to show that κοσμος does not simply designate entities, but a way of being, which is always related to human existence. From the pre-Socratics, there is a five-century leap to Paul and the Gospel of John, in which κοσμος designates the way of human existence that has turned its back on God and dwells far from him. Another leap leads from the New Testament

to Augustine and Thomas; but, contrary to what will become a continual feature of Heideggerian genealogies, the transition from Greek (*kosmos*) to Latin (*mundus*) is in no way thematized, as if the two terms were equivalent. The term *mundus* means, in fact, for theologians, either the totality of the world created by God, or the way of being of men, who place their hearts in the world and not in God. Here it is also a question of reaffirming the mutual belonging of God and world: 'world therefore means the entity in its totality, and precisely in the sense of the decisive "how" in accord with which human existence situates and disposes itself in relation to the entity' (Heidegger 1929, p. 647).

3. The equivalence between *kosmos*, *mundus* and *Welt* is never put in question. Heidegger seems to follow the prevailing opinion among modern philologists, who, on the basis of a fragment by Varro (*Sat. Men.*, 420: *appellatur a caelatura caelum, graece ab ornatu* κοσμος, *latine a puritia mundus*) and a passage by Pliny (N.H., II, 8: *Quem* κοσμος *Graeci nomine ornamenti appellavere, nos eum a perfecta absolutaque elegantia mundum*) tend to consider *mundus*, which also designates, after all, female ornament, a perfect equivalent of the Greek term *kosmos*. Thus, the entry for *mundus* in the etymological dictionary by Ernout and Meillet, published five years after *On the Essence of Ground*, begins, albeit dubiously, with this very equivalence: 'it seems to be the same word *mundus* "adornment", which was chosen to designate the "world", undoubtedly in imitation of the Gr. Κοσμος'.

In 1913, however, Joseph Vendryes published a brief article in *Mémories de la Société de Linguistique de*

Paris in which he questioned this equivalence and drew attention to a likely older meaning of the term *mundus* that linguists and Heidegger seem to ignore and on which historians of religion should instead concentrate their attention. According to the testimonies of Cato (cited by Festus, 144, 11), Varro (cited by Macrobius, 1, 16, 18) and Plutarch (*Romulus,* 11, 2), *mundus* designated a circular aperture that connected the world of the living with the hell of the dead. It was opened three times a year (24 August, 5 October, 8 November) and on those days, considered *religious* for this reason, 'what was hidden and secret in the cult of the Manes gods was brought to light and revealed' and all public activities were consequently suspended. According to Plutarch, the pit that Romulus had dug at the time of the founding of Rome, and into which some first fruits and a handful of earth that each of Romulus' companions had brought from the city they came from, was also called *mundus*. In Rome, therefore, *mundus* did not only designate the circular threshold of the world of the dead; precisely because it connected the dead with the living, it also joined together the past and the present, the country that the founders had left with the new city they had founded.

4. An attempt to trace the genealogy of this concept in order to reconstruct at least its fundamental characteristics seems, at this point, inevitable. In his book on *Ancient Roman Religion* (1966) Georges Dumézil considers such an attempt with some scepticism: 'The notion of *mundus*', he writes, 'is one of the most controversial in Roman religion. Ancient authors seem, in fact, to have mixed various rites and places, and

modern authors have added to the confusion with their arbitrary choices and extrapolations' (Dumézil, p. 310). Immediately following, he summarizes what he considers to be the only reliable information on this enigmatic institution: 'The term *mundus* [. . .] was reserved for two things or types of things. On the one hand, the pit which is forever closed, into which Romulus, at the time of the founding of the city, following a ritual considered Etruscan, had thrown the first fruits "of all that is good from the point of view of custom and from the point of view of nature necessary" and also a little earth from the country from where each of his companions came. On the other hand. A pit (or several pits) that gave access to the underworld, of which the ancient Romans do not seem to have formed coherent representations. The main pit – perhaps the only one – was, according to Festus, "what is called *Cereris mundus*"; this name, confirmed by the existence in Capua of a *Sacerdos Cereris mundalis* (CIL, X 3926), corresponds to a location: the *mundus* was *in sacro Cereris*, that is, without doubt, in a place attached to the temple of the goddess. This *mundus*, usually closed, was opened three times per year' (ibid.).

Curiously, Dumézil does not mention Vendryes' article and can therefore conclude his reference to *mundus* with the peremptory statement: 'It is not possible to reconstruct what our own informants no longer understood; they spoke about it, moreover, sparingly. Etymology does not help: the word *mundus* cannot be explained in the light of Indo-European' (ibid., p. 311). Not without some contradiction, a note at this point refers to an article by an Italian linguist, Evangelisti, who proposes an etymology of the term from the Sanskrit *mandala*.

5. Let us attempt to examine carefully the sources that Dumézil summarizes perhaps a little too briefly. We list them below:

Festus (273 L): 'The *mundus*, as Ateio Capitone says, is usually opened three times per year [. . .]. Cato, in his commentaries on civil law, explains this name in the following way: the *mundus* owes its name to the *mundus* which is above us; in fact, as I have learned from those who have entered it, it has a shape similar to that (of the other *mundus*, that is, the celestial vault). Our ancestors decided that its lower part (*eius inferiorem partem*), as it was consecrated to the Manes gods, should always remain closed, save the days indicated. Those days were considered *religious* for the following reason: our ancestors wanted no official act to be performed at the moment when the occult and hidden things of the religion of the Manes gods were, so to speak, brought to light and revealed (*ea quae occulta et abdita religionis deorum Manium essent, veluti in lucem adducerentur et patefierent*). On those days, therefore, they did not start a battle with enemies, did not mobilize troops, did not hold meetings, did not engage in any official act, except in cases of extreme necessity'.

The mention of a lower part led some to believe that the *mundus* involved a *tholos*, a vaulted well whose shape resembled the vault of heaven and a lower part, which opened only three times per year.

Phaestrus (126, 4): 'What is called the *mundus* of Ceres (*Cereris mundus*), which usually opened three times per year: on the ninth Calenda of September, the third Nona of October and the sixth Ide of November'.

Apuleius' *Cereris mundus*, *Apol.*, 13: 'You judge that for a philosopher to possess a mirror is a sacrilege worse than for a profane person to see the world of Ceres' (*Cereris mundum profane videre*), which is usually referred to the objects kept in the *cista mystica* of the Eleusinian mysteries (thus forcing the sense of 'female ornament' that the term can have in Latin), should instead be restored to the meaning that the same expression has in Festus and implies that it was forbidden for the profane to descend into the *mundus*.

Macrobius (I, 16, 17): 'It was not considered appropriate to start a war [. . .] when the *mundus* (*patente mundo*), sacred to the Father Dis and Proserpina, was open, and they believed it was better to go to war when Pluto's jaws were closed. For this reason, Varro writes: 'When the world is open (*mundus cum patet*), the door of the sad gods and the underworld is open, so to speak; therefore, it is a forbidden act (*religiosum*) not only to engage in combat, but also to take pleasure in military matters, to leave as a soldier, to set sail on a ship, and to take a wife in order to have children'.

Bernese scholium (in *Verg. Buc.*, III, 103): 'According to some, it is the cave with a narrow entrance, but deep down, through which Proserpina was abducted by her father Dis. Others say that the *mundus* was located in the temple of Ceres and that heaven means *mundus*. In other words, for the ancients there was a deep well (*latissimus puteus*), into which a baby (*puer*) was lowered to celebrate sacred rites (*ad sacra celebranda*), in order to know what will be born in the year (*anni proventus*); the round opening (*orbis*) of this well, that is, the top of the circle, measured no more than three cubits'.

The interpretation of this passage has been misled by a restrictive translation of *proventus* as 'agricultural harvest'. The term, which can be used in this sense, more generally means 'that which is born and comes from...' (cf. *superioris temporis proventus*, 'that which comes from the previous time'; *Socratici fetus proventus*, 'the new generation of Socrates' disciples'; *secondi rerum proventus*, 'the favourable outcomes of things'. The verb *provenio* is, moreover, used in an auspicious sense: *Alexandro* [. . .] *simile provenisset ostentum*. In the verse from the *Georgics* (II, 517) which is wrongly cited to prove the meaning of 'harvest' (*proventuque oneret sulcos*), *proventus* clearly means 'rich growth' (the year cannot 'weigh down the soil with the harvest'). The ritual descent of the *puer* into the *mundus* allowed for an omen to be drawn that concerned not only the harvest in the strict sense, but everything new that would be generated in the year. The *mundus* is the place where, between the past and the present, the new that comes into being is experienced.

It is only by referring to this ritual function that we can explain the meaning of the archaic expression *in mundo esse* (*tibi vita seu mors in mundo est*: Ennius, fr. 496), for neither ancient grammarians (who explained it as *in prompt esse* or *pro palam et in expedito accito*) nor modern linguists have been able to find a satisfactory explanation. As Dognini (p. 23) has observed, the expression, which occurs several times in Plautus in auspicious contexts, 'takes on a meaning directed towards the future, as if to ward off bad omens'. Like the *proventus anni* of the ritual, what is 'in the world' is something still hidden, but which is about to happen and which the ritual has the task of bringing to light.

Servius (*Ad Georg.*, I, 38): 'Proserpina was abducted by her father Dis in an underground cave in Sicily [. . .] the cave through which she descended is called *mundus*'.

Servius (*Ad Aen.*, III, 134): 'According to some, altars (*aras*) belong to the celestial gods, fires (*focos*) to the intermediate or marine gods, but worlds (*mundos*) to the infernal gods'.

Plutarch (*Romulus*, 11, 2): 'Romulus summoned priests from Etruria (*ek Tyrrenias*) who were experts in sacred rites. A circular ditch (*bothros*) was dug in what is now the Comizio, and the first fruits (*aparchai*) of everything they would use according to the law or the necessities of nature were thrown into it. Finally, each threw in a small portion (*moran* [. . .] *oligen*) of the earth from which he had come, mixing them together. They call this pit – which is also given the name of heaven (*olympum*) – world (*mundum*). And around this centre, like a circle, he drew the city'.

In a passage from *Fasti* (IV, 819 ff), Ovid invokes a ritual meaning similar to that described by Plutarch, without, however, mentioning the term *mundus*: '*Fossa fit ad solidum, fruges iaciuntur in ima / et de vicino terra petita solo. / Fossa repletur humo, plenaeque imponitur ara / et novus accenso fungitur igne focus. / Inde premens stivam designat moenia sulco*'. The information that the pit was filled with earth and an altar was built on top is missing in Plutarch and has been questioned by scholars, who rightly observe that, according to Servius' gloss on the *Aeneid*, altar and *mundus* are mutually exclusive.

If we consider the ancient sources independently of modern interpretations, the question is perhaps less mysterious than Dumézil seems to think. *Mundi*, as both Festus and Servius' gloss inform us, were places sacred to the gods of the underworld, which ritually connected the world of the dead with that of the living. We know that one of these *mundi* was found in the temple of Ceres, but there must have been others, if Servius refers to *mundi* in general as what corresponds to the altar for the gods of the underworld. These *mundi* were opened three times per year, on days that were *religious* for this purpose and implied the suspension of certain activities, especially warlike ones. Festus briefly describes the form of the *mundus* and the scholium of Bern mentions a rite or one of the rituals that were also performed at the time of its opening. Plutarch also informs us that Romulus, at the time of the founding of Rome, had dug a *mundus* and performed a ceremony on it, as if to signify that founding a city necessarily implied a relation with the dead and with the past (the first fruits offered to the underworld and the handful of earth from the country from which each person came). Whether this *mundus*, whose institution, according to Plutarch's account, was of Etruscan origin, the oldest example from which the other *mundi*, which tradition relates to the abduction of Proserpina to Hades, may have derived, is a historically relevant but not decisive question: in any case, what is common is the vertical relation between the living and the Manes, the sky and the underworld. Both the future of the city, as the Bernese scholium attests, and what it brings each year depend on this relation.

6. If the ancient sources are not actually inconsistent, it is certainly true that modern sources, as Dumézil maliciously suggests, have made them more obscure.

Leaving aside the agricultural interpretations of Warde Fowler and Wagenvoort, who see the *mundus* as a sort of granary where cereal seeds were stored and magical rites were performed to promote crop growth, scholars have focused almost exclusively on the question of whether Plutarch's *mundus* and the *mundi* of other sources are the same thing or should instead be kept separate, as Weinstock, followed by Le Bonniec and Rose, asserts without reservation. No less lively are the discussions on the identity between Romulus' *mundus*, which Plutarch situates in the Comitium, and what the archaeologists believe they had identified on the Palatine Hill, the original site of the *Roman Square* which Festus, in a passage otherwise corrupted, places in *Palatino ante templum Apollinis* and relates it with the founding of the city, writing that it contained all the things *quae solent boni ominis gratia in urbe condenda adhiberi* (Festus, 310 L sg.). While Weinstock, Rose and Dumézil firmly distinguish between them, Du Jardin considers them a single entity, initially located on the Palatine Hill and later moved to the Comitium, and Coarelli, based on a passage by Macrobius that had not been taken into consideration, also identifies them topographically in *umbilicus Romae*.

7. The arguments of the linguists are more useful than those of the archaeologists or anthropologists, as they have attempted to reconstruct the etymology of the term. In the study cited in a footnote by Dumézil, Enzo Evangelisti proposed a derivation of the term *mundus* from the Sanskrit *mandala*, specifically the meaning of 'magic circle', which in *abhicara* practices was usually traced on the ground and serves to delimit the space within which the 'magician' performed his spells, generally in relation to the realm of the dead (Evangelisti, pp. 362–3). While verifying the accuracy of this hypothesis is beyond our scope and expertise, we note, however, that Evangelisti dwells at length on the article by Vendryes, who had early on questioned the underlying meaning of the term *mundus* and its possible etymology. Vendryes rejected (rightly so, according to Evangelisti) the semantic dependence of *mundus* on the Greek *kosmos* and, starting from the meaning of 'endroit profonde, symbole du monde terrestre et ouverture du

monde infernal' (Vendryes, p. 306), he proposed a relation with the Celtic family *dubno* (cf. Irish *domun*, 'bottom' and then 'world'; Welsh *dwfn*, and Breton *don*, 'deep'). A similar semantic evocation, from 'deep' to 'world', would have occurred for the Latin *mundus*, which Vendryes considers to be an allotrope of *fundus* (a term which, meaning depth and abyss, would have been the object of a vocabulary interdiction and thus transformed into *mundus*).

Vendryes' hypothesis was not accepted by linguists for reasons that were not phonetic but purely semantic, since the original meaning of 'depth' did not seem to be compatible, according to Ernout and Meillet, with the older meaning of the term *mundus*, which means 'celestial vault'. However, this objection is not convincing, because the passages by Festus and Plurarch unequivocally affirm the equivalence of the two meanings ('the *mundus* owes its name to the *mundus* above us; in fact, as I have learned from those who have entered it, it has a similar shape'; 'they call this pit – which is also given the name of heaven (*olympum*) – world (*mundus*)').

The Latins knew, that is, a celestial and underground *mundus*: they were, in fact, as the homonymy suggests, the same 'world', divided into two parts corresponding to the circular opening that connected them. It is, therefore, crucial that, from this perspective, the term 'world' acquires an originally vertical dimension, both chthonic and celestial, spatial and temporal. The world is constitutively 'deep', that is, according to Festus' definition of the adjective *profundus* (256, 19), *altus ac fundus*, and this depth – which therefore also implies an upward movement for the Latins – is not only spatial, because it concerns the world of the dead and, in this sense, the sphere of what has been. As Vendryes writes: the opening of a *mundus* 'was in some ways both the taking possession of the land and the establishment of communication with the dwelling place of the Manes, the spirits of the underworld. It was the centre, the navel of the future city, the base on which it would grow and rise. The *mundus* was a concrete and abbreviated representation of the world' (Vendryes, p. 306). The ancient city is founded on the 'world' because men dwell in the opening that unites the celestial vault and the underground vault, the world of the living and the world of the dead, the present and the past, and it is through the vital, ritually maintained relation between these two worlds that it becomes possible for them to orient their actions and find inspiration for the future. This relation is vertical and archaeological, because those who descend into the *mundus* to draw auspices commemorate the gesture with which Romulus founded the city.

Vittore Pisani (Pisani, p. 10) rightly notes that the expression *mundus caeli* appearing in Ennius suggests a distinction and, at the same time, a correspondence with the *mundus* of hell, perfectly equivalent to Cato's *mundus qui supra nos est*. For the Romans, there is a heaven and an abyss above us, just as there is an earth and an abyss below us.

8. In a diary entry from 1953, Hannah Arendt compares Heidegger to a fox, to be precise, a very special fox, who, as is the wont of all foxes, wanted to build a safe den and chose a trap as his lair: 'In his chilling ignorance of traps and non-traps and his incredible experience with traps, he came up with a brand new idea, unheard of among foxes: he built himself a trap as a den' (Arendt, 2007, p. 344). In the guise of gossip, the note actually

contains a valuable indication of the ontology of *Being and Time* and of the very structure of being-in-the-world that defines *Dasein*, *Da-sein*. The *da*, the 'there' that *Dasein* must be, defines its constitutive spatiality, but this spatiality has the form of a being already always thrown into a 'there', a 'here' or a 'there' that *Dasein* has to be, without ever being able to assume them or find a foundation in them. 'The entity whose essence is constituted by being-in-the-world, is its "there". In its most common meaning, "there" indicates a "here" or a "there" [. . .] the existential spatiality of *Dasein*, which determines its place, is founded on being-in-the-world'. The openness of this original spatiality defines *Dasein*, which 'comports its "there" in an original way [. . .] is its openness'. In this sense, in a singularly vicious circle, the ontological structure of *Dasein* is 'such that it must be its own "there"' (Heidegger 1927, p. 87). It must be the very openness to which it is always already given and therefore can never assume as such: '*Dasein* is always already open according to a disposition given as the entity to which *Dasein* is delivered in its being as the being that it, existing, has to be. Open, here, does not mean recognized as such [. . .]. The pure fact of "what is there" shows itself, but the wherefrom and the whither remain in obscurity [. . .]. This character of *Dasein*, veiled in its provenance and destination, but precisely for this reason even more open in itself without shrouding, we call the thrownness (*Geworfenheit*) of this entity in its "there" [. . .]. As an entity delivered to its being, *Dasein* is always delivered to this in such a way that it must always have already been found, found, however, in a finding that does not arise from a search, but from a flight' (ibid., p. 231).

For this reason, the emotional situation of anxiety comes from being-in-the-world itself. What gives being-in-the-world to feel this anxiety is not any of the entities in the world: it is the world itself in its pure and empty openness. 'In the "before what" of anxiety, "nothingness and nowhere" is disclosed [. . .] the before what of anxiety is the world as such. The complete insignificance that is announced in nothingness and in "nowhere" does not mean an absence of the world, but, on the contrary, that the intramundane entity has become so completely devoid of importance in itself that, by virtue of this insignificance of the intramundane, what strikes us is only the world in its worldliness. What oppresses us is not this or that simple presence, nor even the sum total of them [. . .] it is the world itself' (ibid., p. 290). Anxiety, that is, only reveals to man that, in the world into which he has been thrown, he cannot feel at home, he is continually disoriented.

Hannah Arendt's anecdote about the fox that chose a trap as its den reveals its relevance here. The world, understood as a pure openness in a 'there', in a spatiality to which one is irrevocably consigned, is, ontologically, a trap. And that is why, starting in paragraph 70, the analysis of temporality will be entrusted with the task of founding the spatiality of *Dasein*: 'Only because, as temporality, it is ecstatically and horizontally open in its being, can *Dasein* effectively and constantly make an ordered space its own' (ibid., p. 551); 'the essential structures of the constitution of being or *Dasein* [. . .] must be existentially traced back to temporality' (ibid., p. 552). But it is precisely this attempt to trace the spatiality of being-in-the-world back to temporality that will condemn *Being and Time* to remain unfinished.

The entity, which is and must be its 'there' is always already thrown into its openness, is only its openness; it does not allow itself to be constituted temporally. As Heidegger would write without reservation thirty-five years later in the lecture *Time and Being*: 'The attempt in paragraph 70 of *Being and Time* to trace the spatiality of being back to temporality cannot be maintained' (Heidegger 1969, p. 24).

9. What changes if we restore to the term 'world' its original depth? What does it mean for man to 'be-in-the-world' if the world is not simply the totality of entities or that towards which *Dasein* goes beyond and transcends itself and every entity, but first and foremost the subterranean *mundus* into which we must first descend in order to rediscover each time the meaning of our dwelling on earth?

If the original place of man is not the world, but the *mundus*, that is, something *altus ac fundus*, which implies a relation to the dead and with the past, then temporality and memory belong to him constitutively. And the memory that is at issue here is not the faculty of a subject, but the very structure of its being, which keeps it in tension both with the 'high' and with the 'low'. *Mundus patet* means the mode of this opening. The world does not, in fact, open up anxiously onto emptiness and 'nothingness and nowhere', but is, on the contrary, the passage through which the past bursts into the present and, by suspending first and foremost wars and the activities connected with them, suddenly shows itself in the light to guide and decide the actions of men. Those who agree to descend into it encounter, in a singular *nekyia*, what is usually 'hidden and concealed' and draw from these auspicious signs what the future will bring. The world is first and foremost a political reality, for it is on and around it that the city was founded, and it is in it that each of those who contributed to its foundation laid a handful of the earth from which they came and the first fruits of what they considered necessary and worthy of a just and happy life – in other words, their memories and hopes. That it should then take the form of a *latissimus puteus*, that it should be in some way an abyss that can only be opened three times a year, when the two heavens and the two abysses touch and join, shows how difficult it is for men to reconcile hope and memory, what is alive and what is dead – the hope that feeds on memory and the memory that lives on hope.

5

History and Eschatology: Considerations on the Antichrist

1. Idols, writes Bacon, are false notions that occupy and 'besiege the minds of men to such an extent that not only does access to truth become difficult, but even if such access is granted, they will reappear in the very establishment of the sciences, which they will obstruct, unless informed men guard against them as far as possible'. To the four notorious kinds of idols listed in the *Organum* (I.XXXVIII), we propose to add a fifth which we call *idola historiae* and distinguish them from the others, even though it would perhaps be permissible to count them among those that Bacon calls *idola theatri*, because they derive from the 'multiple dogmas of philosophies', which, as we know, produce 'fictitious worlds' and fables as on a theatre stage. We make this distinction because, although they sometimes present themselves as philosophical doctrines, *idola historiae* in reality derive from the theological dogmas of a religion, which, as Marc Bloch wrote, is essentially a religion of historians, whose sacred books commemorate episodes

which are supposedly historical and announce to men a salvation which is inseparable from their adventure in history. The *idola historiae* result from the intertwining of theological and historical categories, which define our conception of history.

They are 'historical idols' because they work on the minds of men, inducing them to isolate human events which, while remaining such, acquire the incomparable privilege of qualifying and determining once and for all the course of history in the sense that, after them, nothing can be as it was before. Precisely for this reason, however, these idols are not simply, as in the invocation of Bacon, false notions, but find their consistency in a reality, namely historical reality, which we cannot superficially define as 'fictitious'. One such event for the west is the birth (or the resurrection) of Christ, after which not only, at least for believers, did the destiny of the human species change completely, but even for those who do not believe in the sacredness of that birth, the succession of historical events was nevertheless constructed chronologically in relation to it. A similar power was felt by those who witnessed – and in some ways still feel – the fall of the Roman Empire, the discovery of America and the French Revolution; more recently, the unique ability to determine the course of history *ex novo* has been attributed, albeit to varying degrees, to the extermination of the Jews, the atomic bomb and the destruction of the natural environment (not to mention the certainly specious attempt to confer such a privilege on the recent influenza pandemic). In some of these examples, the connection with the theological paradigm of the end of the world is so evident that one could speak of a secularization of eschatology, as if calculating historical chronology starting from a theological event forced us to assume as certain or possible the final crisis that was implicit in it.

2. Another of these idols is the Antichrist who, like the Christ he opposes, is a historical being, acting as an earthly power and, simultaneously, something more than a mere man. That this is a theological paradigm is obvious; less obvious is that a particularly astute theologian such as Erik Peterson, who in 1935 had argued with Carl Schmitt on the problem of political theology, could define it as 'the purest form of Christian theology of history' (Peterson 2004a, p. 266). 'A theology', he had already written in 1925, 'that cannot say anything about the Antichrist will not be able to say anything about Christ either'. This thesis, which comes from an author accustomed to measuring his words, should be taken literally.

The term 'Antichrist' (*antichristos*) appears in the New Testament only in the First (three times: 2:18; 2:22; 4:3) and Second letters (once: v7) of John. The context is certainly eschatological (*paidia, eschate hora estin*, vulg. *filioli, novissima hora est*, 'children, it is the last hour!'), and the term appears significantly in the plural: 'as you have heard that the Antichrist is coming, and now many antichrists have come (*kai nyn antichristoi polloi gegonasin*). No less decisive is that the apostle defines the last hour as the 'now (*nyn*)' in which he finds himself: 'the Antichrist is coming (*erchetai*, present indicative)'. Shortly thereafter (4:3), it is specified, if it need be, that the Antichrist 'is now in the world (*nyn en to kosmoi estin*)'. It is important not to forget this eschatological context of the Antichrist, if it is true – as

Peterson, and Barth before him, never tire of reminding us – that any reflection on the last moment of human history is inseparable from Christianity ('a Christianity', writes Barth, 'that is not wholly and entirely without remainder eschatology has nothing to do with Christ' (Barth 1958, p. 298). For John, the Antichrist is the one who in the last hour 'denies that Jesus is the Christ' (that is, the messiah), and antichrists are therefore the 'many' who, like him, 'went out from us, but they were not of us' (2:19), which suggests, not without ambiguity, that the Antichrist ultimately comes from within the *ekklesia*, but does not truly belong to it. As such, he is repeatedly defined as a 'deceiver' (*planos*, literally 'he who leads astray', vulg. *seductor*).

3. Christian theology is permeated by two connected and yet diametrically opposed forces: *oikonomia*, according to which history with its linear time is the place where the salvation or damnation of the human species foreseen by divine providence takes place, and *eschatology*, which takes place at the end of time, when human history is fulfilled and talk of an economy of salvation has lost all meaning. Theologians are divided accordingly, depending on whether they emphasize one or the other, but the choice is not indifferent, because it concerns the very meaning of the messianic event, which is split into an 'already' and a 'not yet', in which economy and eschatology, history and eternity, seem to clash without any possible reconciliation.

For a theologian like Peterson, who is firmly on the side of eschatology, history – the dimension of economy – no longer makes sense in a literal sense, because its time – the *aion houtos*, *hoc saeculum*, this age – has been broken once and for all by the messianic event (the *aion mellon*, the time to come). 'The situation inaugurated in Christ is such that in the the *aion houtos* collides with the *aion mellon*. This means that the productive force, the force that produces history in the *aion houtos*, is at a standstill. What still exists in history is only the last stage of the *aion houtos* before the advent of the *aion mellon*' (Nichtweiss, p. 494). If 'the structure of the world is broken', what is then still being produced in history 'is only a masquerade' (ibid., p. 493) or a 'meaningless enigma' (ibid., p. 495). This senseless counterfeit, this anti-history or no-longer-history is the dominion of the Antichrist. 'The Antichrist is not a man who lives within history. His mystery is due to the fact that he does not appear in history, but in eschatology, in the last days' (Peterson 2004b, p. 139). Insofar as he imitates and counterfeits the kingdom announced by Christ, he is the extreme – albeit vain – appearance of sense that still belongs to history.

4. The place on which the exegesis of the Fathers and theologians on the Antichrist has focused for centuries is not the letters of John, but Paul's Second Letter to the Thessalonians (2:1–12). Although the term does not appear there, the enigmatic character that the letter presents as 'the man of lawlessness' (*ho anthropos tes anomias*) and the 'son of perdition' (*ho yios tes apoleias*) was identified as the Antichrist by Hippolytus, Irenaeus and Tertullian, and later by Augustine. While Hippolytus only briefly mentions the letter, the testimony of Irenaeus and Tertullian shows that in their time there was a Marcionite interpretation of the Antichrist, who was seen as a Christ sent by the demiurge to imitate

and oppose the Christ of the true God. For this reason, both of them – and Justin with them – are careful to emphasize that the Antichrist is not a divine being, but a man – the man, in fact, of anomie, of lawlessness – 'who sums up in himself every error of the devil'.

Paul says of this man, whom he also summarily calls 'the lawless one' (*ho anomos*), that 'he opposes everything that is called God or is worshipped, to the point of sitting in the temple of God, proclaiming himself to be God'. The Antichrist is, therefore, the dark counterpart of Christ's power, a worldly power (one tradition sees him identified with Nero) that seeks to imitate and counterfeit the coming of the Kingdom at the end of time.

The precise correspondence between the Kingdom of Christ and the action of the Antichrist in the world is forcefully stated by Hippolytus. 'Just as our Lord and Saviour Jesus Christ, the Son of God, was foretold as a lion because of his royal and glorious condition, so too did the Scriptures foretell the Antichrist as a lion because of his tyrannical and violent character. The deceiver wants to make himself similar in every respect to the Son of God. Christ is therefore a lion, and the Antichrist is a lion. Christ is king, and the Antichrist is king on earth. And because the Saviour showed himself as a lamb, likewise this man will show himself as a lamb while inside he is a wolf. The Saviour came into the world circumcised, and this man will come in the same way. The Lord sent the apostles to all nations, and this one will likewise send false apostles. The Saviour gathered the scattered sheep, and this one will likewise gather the scattered people. The Lord gave a seal to those who believe in him, and this one will likewise give it. The Lord appeared in human form, and this one will come in human form. The Saviour rose and showed his flesh as a temple, and this one will raise up the temple of stone that is in Jerusalem' (Hippolytus, p. 123).

5. In the Letter to the Thessalonians, however, the man of lawlessness is closely linked to another enigmatic figure, the *katechon*, the one who restrains (also in the masculine form: 'he who restrains'). What is held back is the 'Parousia of our Lord Jesus Christ and our reunion with him': the context of the letter is, therefore, exactly as in the Letter of John, eschatological (shortly beforehand, the apostle invokes 'the righteous judgement of God [. . .] in the revelation of the Lord Jesus with the angels of his power'). Already in the time of Augustine, this power that restrains the final coming of Christ was identified with the Roman Empire (which Paul, according to Augustine, omitted to name explicitly 'so as not to incur the accusation of contempt, wishing evil on the Empire that all believed to be eternal') or with the Roman Church itself, as the First Letter of John seemed to suggest, mentioning the antichrists who 'will come from among us'. Later, both the *Glossa Ordinaria* and Peter Lombard would mention the Church alongside the Empire (both importantly defined by the term *imperium*: *discessio ab utroque imperio* [Peter Lombard, p. 318]).

In any case, if it is the Roman Empire or the Church, the power that restrains is that of an institution founded on a stable law or constitution (anticipating our nation 'state', Tertullian says: *status romanus*, which in his time meant 'the condition of Roman Imperial stability').

In this sense, the Antichrist is 'the prince of this world (*Fürst dieser Welt*)' (Peterson 2004a, p. 256), whose coming in the last days the *katechon* is supposed to delay. As such, he differs from the angels of the nations in the Judeo-Hellenistic tradition, according to which, while Israel is in direct relation with God, each of the other nations has been assigned an angel. Peterson relates these angels to nineteenth-century nationalism and the creation of nation states. Compared to these, the Antichrist, as the prince of the world, represents a superior global power. For this reason, Peterson can write: 'The Antichrist, like Christ himself, will not appear in the East or the West, but will be among us, and it is this being-among-us that will surprise us' (ibid., p. 266). It is worth remembering that in Christian theology, angels are the paradigm of world government. At least since *De coelesti hierarchia*, the vocabulary of angelology has coincided so closely with that of politics that it has been said that Christian theology thinks of politics *sub specie angeli*. 'The concept of the political', writes Peterson, 'must not be defined only on the basis of earthly dominion, but must be thought of together with the heavenly power of angels' (ibid., p. 256). As 'prince of the world', the Antichrist is also 'the prince of the angels of the nations' (ibid.) and, more generally, he is the extreme cipher of angelic power of government, when this, beyond nation states, enters into the perspective of a world government.

6. It is crucial to understand the relation between the power that restrains and 'the man of lawlessness'. This has sometimes been interpreted as a conflict between two powers, in which the meaning of the lawless one or Antichrist 'removes' the restraining power. A more attentive reading shows that the relationship is rather a simple succession. The man of lawlessness will, in fact, be revealed only after 'the apostasy has taken place' (*ean me elthe he apostasia proton, nisi venerit discessio primum*), which cannot mean, as we still read in some New Testament lexicons, that it is the Antichrist who provokes 'desertion' (from the Roman Empire or the Church), but only that this must precede his advent. Even the expression that follows: *eos ek mesou genetai*, 'until (the one who restrains) is removed', does not in any way imply that it is the man of lawlessness who does this: as the Vulgate translation (*donec de medio fiat*) suggests, it is the power that restrains (whether the Empire or the Church) that is removed. The text immediately following is perfectly clear in this sense: 'and then the lawless one will be revealed'. The relationship between the institutional power of the *katechon* and the man of lawlessness is a succession between two worldly powers, one of which is removed and replaced – or passes – into the other. This is, in Paul's words, 'the mystery of lawlessness that is already at work' and which is finally revealed, as if, as the term 'mystery' seems to suggest, the 'lawless one' finally exposed in full light the truth of the power that precedes him.

7. It is impossible to fully comprehend the relationship between the two powers and the two figures in the letter without understanding the structure of time implicit in the eschatological mystery. In the last days, as Peterson never tires of reminding us, the economy is closed and history no longer has any meaning. However, even though, according to the theologian, they have lost their 'history-producing force', events in which men are involved and implicated continue to occur incessantly. It is this paradox of the Christian conception of history that a Catholic jurist such as Schmitt described as 'the eschatological paralysis of every human happening', which only a *katechon*, a restraining power, identified by him as the Christian Empire of the Germanic kings

who inherited Rome, can overcome (Schmitt, p. 44). Peterson prefers to speak in this manner of 'a dialectic of Christian eschatology, according to which the messianic kingdom has already come to pass, but will only find its fulfilment with the second coming of Christ' (Peterson 2004a, p. 262). The temporal structure of eschatological time is, that is, defined by the articulation between an 'already' and a 'not yet'. In the terms of Paul's letter, the 'not yet' corresponds to the *katechon*, which, by delaying the Parousia, prolongs the historical economy, while the 'already' defines the man of lawlessness or the Antichrist, who anticipates the end of time.

'Already' and 'not yet' are, according to all evidence, antithetical terms, and it is the theological articulation of this dichotomy that must be questioned. If the 'already', as suggested by the lexical intuition of Thomas Aquinas' vocabulary, 'makes the present seem like the past and the future seem like the present and attests to the unity of the spirit in one syllable', the 'not yet' inserts a delay into this unity: the present is not yet past and the future is not yet present. At this point the strategy that led theology to this paradoxical articulation becomes clear: it is a matter of saving and holding together at all costs the economy and eschatology, history and the Kingdom, the institution (be it the Empire or the Church) and anomie. All power is ultimately founded on an 'already', on the presupposition of a past that grounds it, and yet it needs a 'not yet' in order to exercise its power. There is still history beyond history, and the end of time inaugurates a sort of supplementary time, in which anything can still happen, on the condition that it no longer makes any sense.

Contra this idea of this senseless supplementary time, it must be stated that the only possible conception of eschatology is one that knows that every moment is the last and that the 'already' and the 'not yet' are not two chronologically distinct moments, as implied in the theological idea of a first and second coming; rather, in the decisive moment – in every moment – the already and the not yet, the *katechon* and anomie, coincide, that is, they fall together. Their coincidence opens the space of the *hour*, of the present that between the 'already' and the 'not yet' had lost its place. The *hour* is not a measurable interval in linear time between a before and after: its time is a gerund, something like 'meanwhile' or 'while', a simultaneity between the two times that theology keeps apart. And that 'while' is the small opening through which, beyond the supposed necessity of economics and the arbitrariness of anomie, it is possible for everyone to grasp their own time each time.

8. If this is true, then the letter contains a doctrine on the fate of all institutional power that should not be overlooked, and it is unsurprising that Peterson saw in it the purest form of a Christian theology of history. According to this doctrine, stable institutional power necessarily gives way to a condition of anomie, in which the constitutionally founded sovereign is replaced by a 'lawless' sovereign who exercises his will arbitrarily. The letter therefore contains a message that concerns us closely, because it is precisely such a 'mystery of anomie' that we are experiencing. State power based on laws and constitutions has been transformed – through a process that began some time ago but is only now reaching its definitive crisis – into a state of anomie, in which the

law is replaced by decrees and measures of the executive power and the state of emergency becomes the normal form of government. It remains that the letter states that once the 'lawless one' has been revealed, 'the Lord will destroy him by the breath of his mouth and will render him inoperative with the manifestation of his presence'. This means that what we are left to think about in the seemingly hopeless situation we are going through is the form of a human community that escapes both the 'not yet' of a power that holds us back with its apparent institutional stability, and the 'already' of the emergency anomie that it presupposes and into which it inevitably converts.

6
Truth, Time and History

And because, not without reason, I have kept with me the statue of truth unveiled by time, and since this statue falls under the present testamentary disposition, I wish that it remain in the house of the eldest son of my descendants, so that there may be a perpetual remembrance of my person, and also so that, by looking at it, all my descendants may remember that the most beautiful virtue in the world resides in truth: for, in the end, this is revealed by time.

Gian Lorenzo Bernini

Αἰὼν πάντα φέρει; δολιχὸς χρόνος οἶδεν ἀμείβειν
οὔνομα καὶ μορφὴν καὶ φύσιν ἠδὲ τύχην.
[Aion brings everything; over time it changes
name, form, nature, and even fortune.]

Palatine Anthology IX, 51 (attributed to Plato)

"Who are you, endowed and adorned with
grace more than due mortal woman?
Why do you not rest? And why the wings at your feet?"

"I am Opportunity, known to few.
The cause of my restlessness? I'm on one
Foot, perched upon a wheel.

Truth, Time and History

I don't fly, nothing competes with my running;
the wings on my feet sustain me
to such speed, when I come, I'm seen by none.

I keep my tousled hair before me, so to
cover my chest and face,
so when I come, none may recognize me.

From behind, my head is shaved
of hair, so he snatches at me in vain
when I've passed him by, or if I turn."

"But tell me: who is she coming with you?"
"Penance, take note and carefully understand:
She who cannot grasp me holds me back.

And you, while wasting time in chatter
and occupied with vain thoughts,
don't you see, and don't you yet understand that
already I have slipped right through your fingers."

Niccolò Machiavelli, *On the Occasion*

Prologue

1. The *Allegory of Truth and Time*, attributed by Roberto Longhi to Annibale Carracci and preserved in the royal collection at Hampton Court, composes on canvas apparently heterogeneous iconographic elements that accentuate its singularity – all the more so if, as art historians suggest, it is an early work. Its singularity does not concern so much the depiction of time as a winged old man, holding an hourglass in his left hand, at which he seems to be staring, and clutching truth in his right hand. What is unusual is that he is emerging from a well, with his left leg still submerged, so that the two figures are resting on the edge of the cistern, as,

Figure 1. Annibale Carracci, *An Allegory of Truth and Time*, *c.*1584–5 © Alamy/Artefact.

albeit differently, are the two female figures in Titian's *Sacred Love and Profane Love*. No less unusual is the truth, which rather than a woman looks like an ephebe with a haloed head, who, turning away from the old man, stares into a mirror held in his right hand (a traditional attribute of both prudence and vanity). His feet rudely trample on a female figure reclining on a low wall, which a mask of ape-like or otherwise beastly face glimpsed emerging from the nape of her neck reveals to be falsehood or deception. This third character, representing falsehood or envy, appears several times in the iconographic tradition of allegory. Unexpected, however, are the two figured on either side: a beautiful woman dressed in sumptuous clothing holding a caduceus and a cornucopia, and a young man with his hands raised, clutching a cup full of flowers in his right hand and ears of corn and poppy bulbs in his left. Scholars refer to a passage by Pliny the Elder, who mentions the presence on the Capitol of two statues by Praxiteles representing Good Fortune and Good Events (*Boni Eventus et Bonae Fortunae simulacra*: XXVI, 23) and attributes to the sculptor Euphranor an effigy of Good Events 'holding a cup in his right hand and an ear of corn and poppies in his left' (XXXIC, 77).

Since the testimony had been reproduced by Cartari in an engraving from his highly successful *Images of the Gods of the Ancients* (1571), which Annibale Carracci was familiar with, the suggestion is certainly plausible. But, this means that the young painter places his allegory in a context in which time and truth are somehow related to the events and vicissitudes – fortunate or unfortunate – of human history.

According to Cartari, the female figure with the cornucopia and the caduceus is not Good Fortune, but Happiness: 'The image of her, that is, of Happiness [. . .] was made by the ancients [. . .] a woman [. . .] holding the Caduceus in her right hand and a cornucopia in her left' (Cartari, p. 394). The image of the well also probably comes from Cartari, who, on the subject of truth, writes that 'she is hidden and cannot be seen by everyone: therefore, Democritus placed her at the bottom of a well, saying that she never comes out unless time, or Saturn her father (as Plutarch says), drew her out on occasion' (ibid., p. 298).

2. In his allegory of truth and time, painted around 1800, Francisco Goya places a female figure seated in the act of writing in the foreground, representing history. The woman, half-naked but with her lap and legs covered, is portrayed in profile, her face turned away

Figure 2. Francisco Goya, *Truth, Time and History*, *c.*1800 © Alamy/Superstock.

from both truth, rigid and stiff in her long white dress, and time, an old man with large white wings, who holds an hourglass in his left hand and with his right grasps the wrist of truth, as if to guide and show off to her. In the sketch found in the Museum of Fine Arts in Boston, certainly more vivid and effective than the finished canvas, currently in the Swedish National Museum, not only are truth and history – as well as time – completely naked, but history in the act of being written turns decisively towards the viewer.

A blue light rains down on the scene from the left, the origin of which is unclear, given that the setting appears to be twilight or nighttime, as suggested by the gloomy flock of owls and bats looming overhead on the right. Some have sought to see in the painting – especially those interpreters who view it, not without a decent dose of anachronism, as an allegory of the Spanish constitution – in the presence of history, an Enlightenment meaning, probably completely alien to Goya, as evidenced by the owls and bats, reminiscent of the nocturnal birds that torment sleeping reason in one of the most famous plates of the *Caprichos*. In any case, the inclusion of history alongside truth and time – no less than the presence of Good Fortune and Good Events in Carracci – deserves some reflection.

3. That history has something to do with time is rather obvious. In the extraordinary cycle of frescoes in the Villa Barbaro in Maser, on the ceiling of the so-called Dog Room Veronese depicted time and history sitting side by side on a sort of sarcophagus. The sullen old man looking askance holds a palm branch (usually an attribute of truth) in his right hand, with which he seems to be fanning himself, and a grim scythe and an arrow in his left. History holds a folio in her right hand (other volumes are resting on the ground at her feet) and with her left index finger she seems to be pointing to something missing. That the object of this peremptory gesture

Figure 3. Paolo Veronese, *Saturn (Time) and Historia*, 1560–1 © Alamy/The Picture Art Collection.

is truth and that history has taken the place traditionally reserved for it is certainly possible, but in any case it is a significant absence. The coupling of history with time has come at the expense of truth, which Aulus Gellius, often cited (*Attic Nights*, XII, 11, 7), defined as *filia temporis*.

When Veronese painted the frescoes in Maser, Machiavelli had long since published his *Florentine Histories*, in which he summarizes the history of Venice in a single chapter, insisting on the weakness of the republic rather than its successes. A letter from the autumn of 1509 to the Council of Ten suggests what these weaknesses were for him, which he never tires of invoking. 'It is the Venetians', he notes not without irony, referring to their territorial losses after their defeat at Agnadello by the League of Cambrai, 'in all these places, of which they are aware, they have a

Figure 4. Jean-Baptiste Boiston, *History Writes on the Wings of Time*, *c.*1786, Paris, Hôtel de Galliffet. Photo © Institut culturel italien, Paris.

painting of St Mark holding a sword in his hand instead of a book. From this it seems that they have learned at their expense that studies and books are not sufficient to hold on to states'. Veronese's fresco, which opens the decoration of the Stanza del Cane in Villa Barbaro, shows Venice seated on the world, holding a cornucopia symbolizing wealth and power, which a woman (Ambition? Envy?) tries unsuccessfully to snatch from her hand. History, figured a little further on with her books, bears witness to this power, which time, with its palm and arrow, can only confirm. And yet, despite the paper aids with which she surrounds herself, she can only point to an absent truth.

In a room at the Hôtel de Galliffet, home to the Italian Embassy in Paris since 1909, a relief above a door depicts history writing on the wings of time. History is represented as a female figure with wide wings spread and flowing hair over her bare breasts. In her left hand she holds a book and in her right she holds a pen with which she writes on the right wing of time, represented naked and almost from behind, with a scythe in his right hand and a circle in his left. As in Goya's painting and Veronese's fresco, history turns her gaze away from time and towards the viewer, presumably observing the events she is transcribing. It is possible that Walter Benjamin, during his visits to the embassy to obtain a visa for his trips to Italy, saw this relief and drew inspiration from it for his famous image of the Angel of History, with his face turned towards the past and his wings prevented from closing by a storm blowing from paradise.

4. A first reading, certainly *facilior*, of Goya's sketch is that time can reveal the truth, according to Seneca's maxim (*veritatem dies aperit*), but without history to record it, this discovery is useless because it remains unknown to men. The implication between time, truth and history is, in reality, more profound. A closer examination shows that the small figure of truth, conventionally represented in front, is mute and expressionless, as if time, whose face is contorted in a terrified grimace, is looking not at truth but at the owls that threaten it, as if powerless to reveal it. If truth needs history, it is not only to be transmitted and known. History too – in the foreground and almost between the two other figures – is naked, an incongruous detail if it symbolized only historiography, the *historia rerum gestarum*, which Veronese's fresco, in fact, dresses in rich drapery. Truth – such is the hypothesis we wish to suggest – is not exhausted in the bare facts that time – understood in a chronological sense – can exhibit. Another nudity is required, this time not mute, in which the facts are presented as *res gestae*, events which have nothing to do with the thoughts and discourses of men, which, according to the etymology of *gerere* proposed

by Varro, must 'support' them, that is, take them on and recognize themselves in them. And for this reason, it is necessary that time itself lay down its sickle and hourglass and transform itself from an inert chronological succession into 'historical' time – that is, in the words of Varro himself, into a time 'which is called "historical" because the things it supports are held together by true investigations – stories – (*quod dicitur 'historikon', quia res in eo gestae veris historiis continentur*)'.

Time, that is, becomes history because of its irreducible relation with truth. And by discovering truth, time transforms itself first and foremost. Indeed, according to our hypothesis, it is possible that it is not time that discovers truth, but truth that gives itself time and transforms it into history. Such is the intricate knot that binds the three naked figures sketched by Goya.

It is worth re-reading the passages from Seneca and Aulus Gellius that are at the origin of the iconographic motif of truth revealed by time, which Bernini's statue in the Borghese Gallery was intended to make canonical. Seneca, in Book II of *De Ira*, touches on it briefly twice, always in relation to the ease with which men allow themselves to be carried away by anger. The cause of anger is, in fact, the perception of having been offended, but since many false accusations appear to be true, it is wise to 'always give yourself time, for time reveals the truth (*dandum semper est tempus, veritatem dies aperit*: II, 22)'. A few pages later, Seneca returns to the subject, recalling that in a trial the evidence and the validity of the oaths are carefully examined, and both parties are granted legal action and all the time necessary (*utique partis dare actionem, dare tempus*), not content with hearing them only once, because 'the truth comes to light all the better the more often it is held in one's hands (*magis enim veritas lucet, quo saepius ad manum venit*: II, 29)'. It is possible that the image of time holding truth in its hands comes from this passage; in both passages, the idea is that time is what we give ourselves, neither yielding readily to the accusers (*ne sint aures criminantibus faciles*) nor examining the words of the witnesses patiently. In both cases, the context is, certainly not without reason, unequivocally judicial.

The passage from *Attic Nights* in which Aulus Gellius states that 'truth is the daughter of time' follows the story of a visit to a philosopher named Peregrinus, who lived in a hovel outside the walls of Athens. Peregrinus used to say that one cannot hope that a sin will remain hidden forever, and he quoted two verses in which Sophocles states: 'Therefore, hide nothing, because time, seeing and hearing everything, reveals everything (*anaptyssei panta*)'. The verb *anaptysso* does not really mean to reveal, but to open, and was used in particular for books: *biblion anaptyssein* meant 'to open a book' in the sense of unrolling the scroll on which the text was written. It is probable that the expression in *De Ira* (*veritatem dies aperit*) comes from Sophocles' tragedy, which has been lost to us but would have been perfectly familiar to Seneca. In any case, the idea is not so much that of uncovering and laying bare, but rather that of opening a book. Time reads the truth in the book of life.

Immediately after recounting the anecdote, Aulus Gellius (an author about whom we know almost nothing, but whose significant work has been handed down to us in numerous manuscripts and has been printed countless times since the incunabulum of 1469) writes cursively: 'Another ancient poet whose name I cannot remember (*cuius nomoen memoriae non est*) said that truth is the daughter of time (*veritatem filiam temporis esse dixit*)'. The confession of this lapse of memory is all the more remarkable given that, in the preface to the *Nights*, Gellius informs us that he wrote his work by collecting his materials precisely so as not to forget them: 'as I picked up a book, whether Greek or Latin, or heard something worth remembering, I took note of it as it came, haphazardly and indiscriminately, according to my own discretion and without regard to genre; then I put it aside to aid my memory, as in a pantry of literary food; so that when I needed a topic or a word that had suddenly escaped my memory, I could easily find it even without having the books from which I had taken it'. The expression, which was to become proverbial, 'truth is the daughter of time' is, therefore, in Gellius' book, an embarrassing exception and is linked not to memory but to oblivion.

5. The notion that historical fact is at least confused is undisputed. This diagnosis, which Lévy-Bruhl stated without reservation in an essay in 1936, has since been confirmed first and foremost by historians themselves. After all, the founder of the *Annales*, Lucien Febvre, whom Lévy-Bruhl does not fail to mention, had already written, in his inaugural lecture at the Collège de France (1933), that historical fact is an 'operational construct'. Contrary to popular belief that 'everything that really happened is historical' and that the historian's task is, therefore, to 'seek the truth of past events', Lévy-Bruhl has no trouble displaying that the notion of historical fact is imprecise, both too broad and too narrow (Lévy-Bruhl, p. 264). Too narrow, because historians necessarily leave out 'a part – and not the least important part – of reality', which is made up not only of events, but also of the representations that people make of them. Not to mention the infinite and anonymous mass of minute yet real events, of which it is impossible to provide an intelligible representation. Too broad, because the more scientific historiography wants to be, the more all events, once ascertained, have the same dignity for it. What is missing is precisely a criterion that allows us to make a selection from the mass of facts in order to qualify some of them as historical. In seeking to identify this criterion in the facts themselves, historians are forced to admit that 'their importance varies according to circumstances, according to the imagination or emotion of witnesses' (ibid., p. 269). The historical fact,

even the most 'eventful' one, such as the assassination of Henry IV by Ravaillac, is not a simple corpus, but acquires its historical value only through a multitude of circumstances that made it possible and escape the attention of the historian, who focuses only on the event that appears to him to be decisive. The time of history appears, on the one hand, as discontinuous, marked by singular events selected more or less arbitrarily, which accelerate or delay its course, but, on the other hand, as consisting in a myriad of facts that are impossible to distinguish and order hierarchically. It is therefore not surprising that the most intelligent – and at the same time most marginal – French historian of the twentieth century, Philippe Ariès, was able to declare that historical fact is simply a construction of the historian.

6. The nexus between time and history was explored by Yan Thomas, a brilliant historian of Roman law, who, in an exemplary study, analysed the relation between historical time and legal time. He did so in relation to a court case, the 1997 trial of Maurice Papon, secretary general of the Vichy government's police prefecture between 1942 and 1944.

'The very factuality of the fact', writes Thomas, 'is not of the same nature for lawyers and historians. For historians, it is immediately apparent. For lawyers, it is subordinate to a previous normative decision. Even before being ascertained, the facts are qualified – qualified, therefore, prejudged. They are thus reduced to a hypothesis necessary for the implementation of a norm: that is, it is verified that the condition on which the sanction connected with the prejudice depends exists' (Thomas, p. 22). If historians and judges can become aware of the difference that divides them in their reference to facts, what is at issue here for Thomas is the very notion of fact itself. 'The usual formula according to which historical truth is not to be confused with judicial truth is too vague [. . .]. In reality, it is not so much the methods which are distinct as the very object they aim at, that is, the truth in question. For some, the fact exists only as a condition of a value judgement that can only be defined legally. For others, the fact is all-encompassing, and the value judgement itself appears as simply one piece of information among others. Many misunderstandings would be avoided, and reflection on the relations between historians and justice would be made easier, if it were understood that the boundary between history and law does not only oppose a judgement on reality to a value judgement, but crosses the fact itself, which, in law, is necessarily predetermined' (ibid., p. 23).

It is possible that, if Thomas had accounted for Lévy-Bruhl's considerations, the opposition would have been less drastic. Both historical and legal facts are constructed, and this circumstance is even more significant in that the construction itself is a historical fact. From the moment he became capable of speech, man has always dealt with historical constructions and never with bare facts (bareness itself is, moreover, a legal category, which distinguishes the *quaestio facti* from the *quaestio iuris*). However, we are particularly interested in the implications of this awareness for the conception of time and truth, which is one of the essential themes of Thomas' investigation. The Papon trial concerned crimes that would have been time-barred had a 1964 law not made crimes against humanity, of which Papon was accused, imprescriptible. It is on this particular historical and temporal situation of an imprescriptible crime that Thomas focuses his reflection. Time in law is not a neutral fact, so to speak, but is constructed each time according to regimes of temporality that act as if time were other than what it is. 'Time in law is always constructed – and constructed precisely in the contrary sense to concrete experience' (ibid., p. 28). Thus, in annulment, the event, even though we know it happened at a certain time, is as if it had not happened, '"retroactivity" transports the event to another time, prescription and amnesty erase the past, imprescriptibility maintains the past in the present' (ibid.). In this way, it is the very relation of human beings to their historical situation that is altered. In the case of the Papon trial, 'everything happens as if, on a legal level, we all became contemporaries of his imprescriptible crime'. The historical duration, according to which that act belongs to the past, is suspended in a sort of abstract atemporality. We are contemporaries of a crime that we cannot experience, whose truth we cannot witness or remember, and yet we cannot forget because it cannot pass.

7. With regard to these unforgettable crimes, Thomas invokes, at a certain point, a legal procedure that no longer exists in modern codes, but which throughout the Middle Ages and the *Ancien Régime* was one of the most significant chapters in the legal history of the West: *damnatio memoriae*. The punishment for some of the most serious crimes, such as treason or lese-majesty (but also, in the case of the Inquisition, heresy), meant that the memory of the accused and their actions was purely and simply erased. Not only was their name no

longer to be mentioned, but it had to disappear from all documents, of whatever nature, in which it appeared (*abolitio nominis*); as for the legal consequences of their actions (except for the crime in question), it was as if they had never taken place. If the imprescriptible crime is a fact that cannot be forgotten, in *damnatio memoriae* something must no longer be remembered, it becomes immemorable.

It is worth reflecting on the particular relationship between time, truth and memory that is in question here. The *damnatio* is a kind of anti-history. History, which in Veronese's fresco held its folio tightly and pointed towards truth, must throw away or hide the books in which she recorded events for posterity. That name and that face must remain without history. Truth has nothing to do with memory; it is not revealed by time and in time, but rather expunged and erased by time. Even the dead are not safe from *damnatio*: their corpses, as in the synod of 897 against Pope Formosus, are exhumed from the tomb, tried and thrown into the Tiber. At issue is a truth that is for some reason so burning that it must be erased from memory at all costs – a task that is probably impossible. In any case, the relationship between truth, time and memory is once again decisive.

8. The nineteenth century, which some have defined as the 'century of history' closes with three brilliant liquidations of history: Nietzsche's second *Untimely Meditation*, Péguy's *Clio* and Proust's *Recherche*. In both Proust and Péguy, who straddle the border of the twentieth century, the liquidation is carried out in the name of memory. Clio, the muse of history, already defined as 'the teacher of errors; the mother of impostures' (Péguy, p. 32), 'chewing words with her historical teeth; murmuring, muttering. . .' (ibid., p. 95) for the historian, who deals with 'visible, external, apparent articulations: coarse', she opposes the memoirist and the chronicler, who 'when they talk about the Commune, or the wars, or the Empire, do not set out to tell you the story. Every piece of wall, every stone is for them a text and a subject of remembrance' (ibid., p. 289). While in the eyes of the writer of history the real event 'becomes almost instantly a historical event [. . .] less than nothing, ashes' (ibid., p. 32), the chronicler sticks to reality and his own time. The time of history 'always carries the scythe on the same shoulder' and 'always reaps in the same direction'. His is 'the unilateral law par excellence', in which 'all is lost and nothing is gained [. . .] all is lost and *nothing is created*' (ibid., p. 165). The truth of this lost time – this is Proust's teaching – appears only in the epiphanies of memory, of a memory that is resolutely non-archival, much closer to Péguy's chronicler, 'eager to live literally another time, at this point abolished and happy' (ibid., p. 290).

9. That the truth has a constitutive relation with memory is one of the most essential teachings of Plato's philosophy. This relationship is so intimate, that it can be said that memory is the very form of knowledge. For this reason, truth necessarily has to do with time and the past. 'If he has not learned them (true opinions) now in this life', says Socrates of the servant to whom he recalls the theorems of geometry, 'it is evident that he must have possessed and learned them at some other time' (*en alloi tini chronoi*: *Men.*, 86a). But what this 'other time' is, remains unclear, because Socrates simply suggests that the time in question is the one 'when he was not yet a man' (*ho chronos ot'ouk en anthropos*). The enigmatic expression, which seems to evoke an ancestral time, is clarified immediately afterwards as referring to the totality of time: 'Has he not known them for eternity (*ton aei chronon*, for all time)? It is clear, in fact, that he is or is not a man for all time' (*ton panta chronon*: ibid.). But when and how can we say that we experience time as a whole if, as the repetition of *aei* suggests ('if the truth of beings (*alethia* [. . .] *ton onton*) is always *aei*, in the soul'), is it not simply a matter of infinite duration? What is the other time of truth and memory? How is the 'truth of beings' in the soul?

10. As Mazzarino has noted, classical historical thought recognizes two families of terms to express time: one that derives from the Latin *saeculum* and the Greek *chronos*, which indicate a countable time, and the other which derives from the Latin *aevum* and the Greek *aion*, which correspond to a lived time. The observation of the historian is certainly correct, but the definition of the two families of words can be further refined. The original meaning of *aion*, as Benveniste has shown from an etymological vantage, has nothing to do with time, but with life or vital force (in Hippocrates, with the spinal cord, the seat par excellence of this force). If Homer can put the invocation 'may *aion* abandon me' (*me kai lipoi aion*) into the mouth of the wounded Sarpedon, it is clear that simply translating 'may time abandon me' would not make sense. It would be no less improbable to translate Aeschylus' verse (*Ag.*, 544) '*tis plen theon / apant'apemon ton di'aionos chronon*' as 'who, except the gods, is free from misfortune for all time?'

Not even the translation 'duration of life' proposed by some (Philippson) is completely unsatisfactory. H. M. Keizer, in a well-documented study, has established that not only does the term *aion* originally refer to life, but that even when it seems to acquire a temporal meaning, in reality the vital dimension continues to be a constitutive presence. The scholar does well to demonstrate that the authors who have preceded her oscillate between the two meanings without managing to bring them together. The fact is that, while for the modern ear the semantic spheres of life and time are clearly distinct, it would seem that for the Greeks the very structure of life is intimately temporal, and *aion* refers precisely to this irreducible coincidence of the two terms. It is in this sense that Aeschylus, in whose plays *aion* seems to acquire a temporal nuance (in *Suppl.*, 574 and 582, it is defined as 'incessant' and 'long'), he can speak of the *symphytos aion* (*Ag.*, 107), a 'congenital or innate [*connaturato*] *aion*' that the gods have granted to men. It is this innate nature of time in life that Aristotle expresses when he writes that 'the fulfilment (*telos*) that embraces and contains the time of each life is called *aion*' (*to periechon tou tes ekastes zoes chronou*: *De Coelo*, 279a, 22). If we recall the strong meaning that the term *periechon* has in Aristotle (1023b, 26: 'that which contains so that the things contained form a unity'), it is not difficult to understand how *aion* expresses an inseparable unity of life and time. The perception of one's own life coincides with the perception of time and, vice versa, perceiving time means living. *Aion* can express this unity because, as Keizer has demonstrated through a meticulous lexical analysis, unlike *zoe* and *bios*, the term designates life defined as a whole and, unlike *chronos*, which is time dilated and measurable, means 'time as a whole' (*Aion* is a whole of time: Keizer, p. 36). At the point at which we perceive life as a whole, time is also arrested and is fulfilled. The whole of time and the whole of life coincide in *aion*.

The statement that follows the quoted passage from *De Coelo* allows us to understand how this meaning, initially referring to human life, gradually extended to the life of the cosmos and thus acquired a meaning closer to our notion of time: 'According to the same discourse', writes Aristotle, '*aion* is also (called) the fulfilment of the whole heaven and the fulfilment that embraces and contains all time and infinity (*ton panta chronon kai ten apeirian periechon telos*). It received its name from being eternal (*aei*), immortal and divine'.

But, even in this case, *aion* designates the totality of *chronos*, of measurable time and life, which the Latins will express with the term *aeternitas*. In the treatise of the third Ennead *On Aion and Chronos*, Plotinus emphasizes this aspect in writing that *aion* is a life 'all together (*omou panta*)', 'immobile (*atreme*)', and 'which remains in the one and in relation to the one' (*en eni kai pros en estosan*: III, 7, 10). And Boethius' definition of *aeternitas* (V, 6) is: *interminabilis vitae tota simul et perfecta possessio*, 'the complete and simultaneous possession of an immeasurable life'. In this sense, Cartari contrasts it with perpetuity, which 'even though it never ends, does not possess its infinite life entirely in the same point; which is characteristic of Eternity according to Boethius' (Cartari, p. 17).

Ancient lexicons, such as those of Apollonius the Sophist and Hesychius, agree in defining the primary meaning of *aion* as 'the

Figure 5. *Aion*, *Mellon*, *Enestos*, *Paroichemenos*.
Mosaic, House of Aion, third century CE.

life of man' (*ho bios tou anthropou*; in Hesychius the temporal meaning is listed in the second place: *hot es zoes chronos*). The *Etymologicum Magnum*, from the Byzantine period, emphasizes the substantial irrelevance of the term to time with a quotation from Gregory of Nazianzus: '*aion* is not time nor a part of time, because it is not measurable'. However, it is in Christian authors that the temporal meaning tends to become more precise. After declaring that *aion*, as it is not measurable, is not time, the same lexicon records the meaning of a millennium-long period that marks the history of the world: 'each of the seven *aiones* from the creation of heaven and earth to the resurrection of men is called *aion*' (Keizer, p. 20). Both Hesychius and the *Etymologicum Magnum* mention the passage from Hippocrates (*Epid.*, VII, 22) in which *aion* seems to be identified with the spinal cord (*myelos*): 'as Hippocrates says, a man such in the *aion* (*nosesas ton aiona*) died within a week'.

11. It is because it expresses this complete unity of time and life that *aion*, unlike *chronos*, is represented as a young man (*iuvenis* is etymologically related to *aion* and *aevum*). In Roman frescoes and mosaics the naked young man is surrounded by – or more often holds in his hands – an oval or circle representing the zodiac and the

celestial sphere, again an image of the totality of time and life. It is significant that *aion* – immobile time – is often related to the passing of time, sometimes depicted as the seasons crossing the zodiacal sphere and, in a villa in Antioch's mosaic, as three seated male figures that a caption at the bottom unequivocally identifies as 'the times' (*chronoi*). Their identity is further clarified by another caption above their heads that reads: *Mellon, Enestos, Paro(i)chemenos*, future, present and past. To their right, *Aion*, eternal time, partially covered by

Figure 6. Aion, god of eternity, standing with the circle of the Zodiac and Tellus (Gaia) with the genii of the four seasons (symbols of the cycle of time). Mosaic from the Roman villa in Sentinum (Sassoferrato), 200–250 CE.

Figure 7. *Kairos* (Roman work after the original by Lysippos), *c.*350–330 BCE
© Alamy/Heritage Image Partnership Ltd.

damage to the mosaic, raises the zodiac circle with his right hand, of which the three *chronoi* are the mobile aspect that passes incessantly.

In another mosaic, originally in Sentinum (modern Sassoferrato) and now in the Glyptothek in Munich, *Aion* is a naked young man holding the zodiac circle with his right hand.

It has been correctly observed that the circle that *Aion* holds with his right hand is, in truth, a Möbius Strip, in which the outer surface just above the god's head inexplicably passes into the inner surface to reveal the signs corresponding to the months that mark the passing of time. The ancients, happier than us in this respect, regarded *Aion*, the totality of time, as something natural and inseparable from the cosmic order, of which mortals are a part. This is why Gaia, the earth, is depicted in the foreground of the Sassoferrato mosaic, testifying to the closeness between *Aion* and the time of nature and the cosmos.

And yet, even for the ancients, approaching the naked god in the middle of the celestial wheel to perceive time as a whole must not have been so discounted, if they knew of a figure whose arduous and risky task was precisely that of grasping the propitious moment.

12. The iconography of *kairos* that has been handed down to us, as well as the descriptions in ancient sources, derive from a bronze statue by Lysippos, which the artist is said to have sculpted as a monument to Alexander.

The original has been lost, but we have descriptions of it in two epigrams by Posidippus (fourth century BCE) and Ausonius (fourth century CE) and a relevant description in a mutilated relief from Trogir dating to the first century BCE and another perfectly preserved in the Museum of Antiquities in Turin from the second century CE. Here *Kairos* is represented as a naked, winged young man, holding a crescent-shaped razor in his left hand, on which a two-plated balance hangs. A tuft of hair falls from his forehead onto his face, while the back of his head, as the sources specify, is bald. His feet, which are balanced on a narrow ledge, are also winged. The representation of his right hand is unusual, with his index finger and little finger extended over the right plate of the scales in the apotropaic gesture of the horns. 'It is not clear whether this is to balance it or, as seems more likely, to unbalance it, or to determine the limits of its oscillation' (Solimano, p. 205). Later sources, such as Callistratus' *Descriptions* (fourth century CE) and a letter by Tzetzes (twelfth century), add the detail that the young man keeps his feet on a sphere or a wheel (as depicted in an eleventh-century relief from Torcello, in which *Kairos* is seen walking on

Figure 8. *Kairos* between *Metanoia* and *Praevidentia*, twelfth century. Torcello, Santa Maria Assunta Cathedral.

two winged wheels). Ausonius' epigram also mentions the figure of a woman, Metanoea or repentance, who accomplishes the occasion and punishes those who have failed to seize it ('when I fly away, this remains; those I left behind hold it back'; in the relief at Torcello, it is depicted as a woman supporting her head with her left hand, in the traditional position of melancholy).

13. *Kairos* becomes the Latin *occasio* and in this way the young man is transformed into a maiden (already in Ausonius a 'rare goddess known to few' (*sum dea quae rara et paucis Occasio nota*). A fable by Phaedrus describes with his usual poignancy the 'brief occasion of things', defining it as 'image of time' (*effigiem Temporis*): 'Running with wings, suspended on a razor / naked body, bald with a hairy forehead / if you catch it, you hold it, but once it has fled / not even Jupiter could recapture it / and it signifies the brief occasion of things (*occasionem rerum significat brevum*). / So that lazy delay would not prevent effective action / the ancients forged such an image of time'.

The interpretation of *kairos-occasio* as the fleeting and precarious moment of decision which must not, under any circumstances, be missed, remains vague if we do not consider not only all the details of the images handed down to us, but also the descriptions of literary sources. In the first place, the tuft of hair on the forehead and the bald spot on the back, a motif so constant that it must have been inherited from representations of fortune. The tuft, suggests Posidippus, is 'to be grasped by those who come towards me (*hypantiasanti labesthai*)', while baldness means that 'once I have overtaken them, none will be able to grasp me from behind (*exopithen*)'.

Ausonius, who agrees on the meaning of the baldness (*ne tenear fugiens*), explains the tuft covering the face of opportunity as her desire not to be recognized (*agnosci nolo*). In any case, it is certain that opportunity can only be seized from the front and never from behind, and that the mistake that leads to regret consists precisely in trying to seize it from behind as it passes quickly, instead of coming towards it (*ypantiasianti*, *antao*, that is to say, 'meeting face to face'). That is, it is a gesture contrary to that of the historian according to Péguy, who seeks to grasp the past, so to speak, from behind. What is in question in *kairos*, on the other hand, is a particular experience of time, which does not let it pass, but goes out to meet it and arrests it. Repentance, from this perspective, is not so much the consequence of the inability to grasp *kairos*, but rather what causes it. To repent means to separate within oneself a before and an after, and the repentant man is always consequently split between a future that rushes in and an irrevocable past. For this reason, as in the relief at Torcello, it is represented as an old man stretching his hands in vain towards the opportunity that is quickly slipping away. That old man is the historian, for whom the past no longer contains any possibility, any opportunity, but only the sadness and *poenitentia* of the irrevocable. To this linear time in perpetual flight, *kairos* contrasts the experience of an interruption and a suspension, in which life is *tota simul* in the present and, as the Stoics said, all times are contracted and suspended at one point (*omnium temporum in unum collatio*).

14. Repentance, *metanoia*, is a figure of memory, but of a memory that always arrives *post-festum* and cannot

grasp the past event as something alive. There is, however, another figure of memory, which does not record in its archive what has happened once and for all, but remembers what has not yet fully happened and therefore does not cease to happen. This memory does not try to grasp the past from behind and from the rear, but sees it suddenly coming towards it, face to face. And if, with a gesture of the hand, it grabs the tuft that the occasion offers it, it can then act on the past and, so to speak, modify it, making – as has been suggested – 'the unaccomplished (happiness) accomplished and the accomplished (pain) unaccomplished'. Such a memory truly is, in the words of Posidippus, *kairos ho pandamator* 'lord and tamer of all', and in no case can it give way to repentance. His is 'the other time' of which Plato spoke, which is not in the past, but in the age – in the *aei* – of the present, in which it is possible to grasp not the reality of facts, but their truth.

15. It is possible that the idea of a suspension of time is present in the image of the scales suspended on a razor's edge, so characteristic of the reliefs of Trogir and Turin. The metaphor of the razor derives from a passage in the *Illiad* (X, 173–4) that has become proverbial, in which Nestor states that 'everyone is on a knife edge (*epi xyrous istatai akmes*), facing either a terrible death for the Achaeans or life'. Just as in the Homeric verses in question, what is in question is not a possibility of deciding, so too the scales poised on a sharp blade are not so much an image of decision as that of the impossibility of deciding (the fingers outstretched in an apotropaic gesture perhaps express this very impossibility). The Stoics said that the life of man caught up in the flight of

chronoi falls into incessant deferral, is always lacking and imperfect (*maxime vitae vitium est, quod imperfecta sempre est, quod aliquid in illa differtur*). *Kairos* does not leave this time for an eternal elsewhere: rather, it is the grasping of time within time, kept until the last moment on a razor's edge and poised on a sphere. And if time always marks a disconnection of life from itself, *kairos* grasps this very disconnection. Only in this way can it find itself face to face with the occasion, recognize its true appearance despite the tuft of hair covering its face, and abruptly arrest it, without letting it slip incessantly through its fingers as happens to those who are condemned to repentance. It is not time that reveals the truth, but, on the contrary, it is the truth that exposes and lays time bare.

Kairos is neither *chronos* nor *aion*, neither chronological time nor eternity, which pass into one another in a perpetual oscillation. A passage from Aristotle (*An. Pr.*, I, 36; 49b, 35) emphasizes this heterogeneity between *kairos* and *chronos*: '*Kairos* is not an opportune time (*chronon deon*). In fact, *kairos* belongs to the god, while for *chronos* it is not so, because for the god nothing is opportune'. The commonplace view that sees *kairos* as merely the decision of the opportune moment is called into question here. In *kairos*, *aion* and *chronos*, the divine time of the cosmos and fleeting time coincide, that is, they fall together. Into what? Into the contingency of memory and of a gesture, by definition undecidable and true. *Kairos* is a divine gesture, it is always the sudden opportunity for a gesture that must not be missed. The gesture can also be the work of each individual, as in the passage from the *Republic* (370b), in which Socrates recalls that 'if you let the *kairos* of your work (*ergou kairon*) pass you by, you will be ruined'. It is this intimate connection between time and human action that Isidore summarizes dramatically in his *Etymologies*, writing that: 'Time is not comprehensible in itself, but only through human actions (*Tempus per se non intelligitur, nisi per actus humanos*)'. Time in itself reveals nothing, gives nothing to comprehend: rather, it needs to be discovered and understood, that is, grasped. This is why *Occasio* becomes Fortuna, also depicted as a winged goddess standing on a sphere with a thick tuft of hair on her forehead and bald at the back, sometimes holding a scale. The name Fortuna comes from *fors*, *forte*, *fortasse*, that which is uncertain, but in that 'perhaps [It. *forse*]', like each of us dwells and

Figure 9. Andrea Mantegna, *Occasio et Poenitentia*, *c.*1500.

gives itself. Fortune or opportunity, what is essential is that we cease to question fate and destiny, and grasp, in gesture and memory, the brief moment, before and beyond any decision and possible regret. Otherwise, as the winged maiden in Ausonius says and as a Mantuan fresco from the school of Mantegna effectively shows, 'even you, while you ask, while you linger questioning, realize how I slip through your fingers'.

7
The Language that Remains

What then remains? Language remains.
H. Arendt in conversation with G. Graus

1. *Relic* [*Reliquia*] means remnant. The *Lives of Saints* provides us with information concerning the Christian cult of relics. We see that on 30 June 446, upon the death of Hypatios, abbot of the monastery of Rufinianai, near Constantinople, the crowd of faithful 'tore apart the funeral bed to take away some of the remains of his clothes: one cut the shroud with a knife, another tore off his beard hair' (Kaplan, p. 20). Almost a century later, when the body of Theodosius, hegumen of a Palestinian monastery, was laid out, 'one could see the crowd rushing in droves, monks and lay people together; some rushing to touch the body to obtain a blessing, others tearing clothes that covered it and plucking the hairs of his sacred beard, each wanting to have something that had belonged to him to rekindle the flame of memory' (ibid.). Upon the death of Alypius the Stylite, 'the women came to blows, weeping over the remnants (*leipsanon*)

of the saint, to prevent the body from being taken away and thus being deprived of the blessing' (ibid.). Four centuries later, a disenchanted spectator described the attempts of the faithful to take away something of the holy relics of Nikon the Metanoeite as 'acts of gross stupidity' (ibid.).

The most ancient attempt to establish a theological basis for the veneration of relics is the treatise *De laude sanctorum* by Victricius, Bishop of Rouen (late fourth century). The base of his argument – in which the material and the spiritual seem to merge – was the claim of a consubstantiality and almost, as he says, 'concorporeality' between the body of Christ and that of the devotees and saints, who form themselves as a single mass and a single genus. 'Let us gather, according to the suggestion of scripture, the single mass of corporeality (*unam corpurolentiae massam*) [. . .] we must know, dear brothers, that men are not separated by nature, but only by time, place, action and thought. Diversity is foreign to unity, but unity spreads everywhere without suffering diminution. And if the eyes of the mind see that there is one body for all men (*omnium hominum unum corpus esse*), it follows that for those who live in Christ and in the Church, we must believe for the same reason that there is one substance of flesh, blood and spirit. Just as, through the sacrament of baptism, we are joined to the divine spirit, so for this very reason are our bodies united by the bond of faith; how can we doubt, then, that the apostles and our martyrs also merited perfect and absolute unity? [. . .] It remains, therefore, that they are all in the Saviour. For those, in fact, in whose faith there is nothing dissimilar, everything is common in the truth of God. Through justice they become companions of the Saviour, through prudence they become emulators, through the use of concorporeal arts, through the consanguineous blood, through the host, consorts of the eternity of the cross' (Victricius, pp. 79–80).

Decisive, in this consubstantiality, is the full presence of God in every part of the saints' bodies. In the smallest fragments of the saints' bodies (*in minutiis sanctorum*) 'the truth of the whole passion of the body (of Christ)' must be considered present (ibid., p. 83). 'We declare with all faith and all authority that there is nothing in relics that is not full. The limbs have integrity, where medicine has integrity' (ibid., p. 84). And it is this presence of the whole in the part that constitutes the relic as such: 'Why do we call them relics? Words are images and signs of things. Blood and mud are placed before our eyes. We – as if moved by the impression of a living word – mark them with the names of relics, because it is not possible to do otherwise. Affirming the whole in the part (*totum in parte dicendo*), we do not place them before the eyes of the body, but open the eyes of the heart [. . .]. We have shown that the whole can be in the part. We must not discuss their smallness here. When we say that, as with the genus, nothing dies in sacred bodies, we mean that what is divine knows no diminution, because it is everything in everything. And where there is something, there is everything (*ubi est aliquid, ibi totum est*)' (ibid., p. 85).

The remnant – the relic – here acquires a technical meaning, which distinguishes it from a simple part of a body. The relic is a part that stands for the whole, which has the same substance and power as the whole and, indeed, in some ways exceeds it. Hence its ability to heal and perform miracles: 'Healing is found no less in the parts than in the whole [. . .]. What heals, lives and what lives, is in the relics. The apostles and the martyrs heal and purify. They are therefore bound to the relics by the bond of all eternity' (ibid., p. 88).

The situation regarding relics is more complex with regard to the body of Christ. Since Christ ascended into heaven with his entire body, he cannot have left any bodily relics. Hence the proliferation of relics by contact, from fragments of the Cross, scattered throughout Christendom, to the veils and shrouds that touched his body (the *mandylion*, which Christ is said to have given to the king of Edessa, and the *Veronica* which a holy woman brought to Rome to heal the emperor Tiberius). Proof of the stubborn imagination of theologians and priests is their identification of those fragments of Christ's body that may have detached from him before the Ascension: the foreskin for his circumcision (preserved both in Conques and in the Lateran, but Calvin in his time enumerated thirteen places designated for this remnant) and the teeth of the baby Jesus, jealously guarded by the monks of San Medardo, As for the blood that flowed from his wounds at the passion, the ampoules containing it, placed in precious reliquaries, are dispersed, to remain only in the west, in the churches of Bruges, Mantua and Bologna.

It is against these relics that Guibert of Nogent composed his *De pignoribus sanctorum* (early twelfth century). The only presence of the body of Christ is in the Eucharist, and because of this it was not possible for him to leave relics, because his intention was 'to make us pass from his original body to his mystical body and in this way gradually instruct us in understanding divine simplicity' (Platelle, p. 113). In any case, the choice of the legal term 'pledge [*pegno*]' is significant: relics realize here and now in a material object the presence of the saint's body in the heavenly sphere, just as a pledge guarantees the satisfaction of the creditor's expectation. Here too, a part is worth as much as the whole, which it anticipates and assures.

2. Even in funeral rites remnants are in question. And in at least two senses: the *eidolon* or spectre of the dead and the corpse. The first effect of death is, in fact, to fragment the unity of the living person into a series of elements or remnants that funeral rites must somehow recompose. The most disturbing of these is the phantasm or image of the dead (the *larva* of the Latins, the *eidolon* and *phasma* of the Greeks, the *pitr* of the Indians, the *ba* of the Egyptians), a vague and threatening being that remains in the world of the living and returns in its own likeness to the places it frequented. The purpose of funeral rites is to transform this uncomfortable remnant into a propitious ancestor, who lives in a separate world and with whom ritually defined relations are maintained. It is therefore a question of honouring and, simultaneously, eliminating and hiding that other embarrassing remnant, the corpse, by washing it, perfuming it, dressing it and finally bury, incinerate or abandon it to birds of prey. If it is true, as Malamoud observed, that funeral ceremonies have no other reason for being than to provide a 'meticulous and determined' answer to the question 'how to dispose of the corpse?', it is equally true that, despite meticulousness and determination, it is impossible to completely eliminate every remnant. For this reason, an alternative solution to the elimination of the corpse is its mummification, which pretends that the

dead is still alive, that the remains are not actually such. Or, in the Christian context, the transformation of the mummy into an integral relic, which has its designated place under the altar of the Eucharist.

In any case, it is certain that funeral rites concern the way in which human societies resolve, as far as possible, the problem of the remains of what is no longer alive. It is in this sense that they are fundamentally concerned with the way in which people deal with and organize their relation with what has been, coming to terms with their own past.

3. In 1934, Bergson published the essay *Le possible et le réel* (The Possible and the Real), in which he advances the thesis, surprising at first glance, that the possible does not precede the real, but presupposes it, as a sort of retrospective projection of the present into the past. He begins with the example of the artist who composes a work. To say that this work, since it has been created, was possible, is to ignore that only because a man of genius appeared at a certain point and composed it, we can delude ourselves that it was already possible. In fact, it became so 'retrospectively or retroactively' only from the moment it was realized. For this reason, we cannot say that it was already possible in the past, but only, using that curious 'future in the past' expressed in the future perfect tense, that it 'will have been possible' only today, once it has been produced. To the objection that this means maintaining that the present has the power to introduce something in the past, that 'action goes back in time and leaves its mark backwards', Bergson responds that he never claimed that something real can be inserted into the past, but only 'that something possible can be

situated in it, that indeed the possible is situated in every moment of the past' (Bergson 2011, p. 13). 'As reality is produced, unpredictable and new, its image is reflected behind it in an indefinite past. In this way, it seems to us to have been possible since time immemorial, whereas it is only at this precise moment that it begins to have always been so; this is why I said that its possibility, which does not precede reality, will have preceded it once reality has been produced. The possible is therefore the mirage of the present in the past [. . .]. It is as if, seeing our own image in the mirror in front of which we stand, we claim that we could have touched it if we had remained behind it. Judging thus that the possible does not presuppose the real, we admit that realization adds something to simple possibility, that the possible was already there from the beginning, like a kind of phantasm waiting for its hour, which would become reality through the addition of something, through some unknown transfusion of blood or life. We do not realize that the opposite is true, that the possible implies the reality that correspond to it with something added to it, since the possible is the combined effect of reality once it has appeared and a device that rejects it backwards' (ibid., pp. 13–14).

If we put aside the metaphors that Bergson makes use of in his essay (the mirror, the reflected image, the mirage), we could say perhaps with greater precision that the possible is something like a remnant of the present in the past. Just as there are relics of the past in the present, so there are remnants of the present in the past. This means, in other words, that reality constitutively exceeds itself, that there is always something in the present that we cannot grasp and live, and which therefore remains unexperienced and unlived. It is this remnant of reality that is rejected into the past as something still possible, just as, in Freud's theory, trauma that the conscious mind cannot accept is repressed into the unconscious as an unwieldy remnant, which will return to consciousness in pathological forms before finally emerging in memory. This excess of reality, this remnant that the present leaves behind, has, in fact, two forms or two faces: the first is the possible, which Bergson rightly shows does not precede but follows reality; the second is memory.

4. That there is a kind of secret kinship between memory and possibility has been demonstrated by Benjamin. In a note in the *Passagenwerk*, he writes that 'in memory we have an experience that prevents us from conceiving of history in a fundamentally atheological manner' (N8,1). 'What knowledge has "established" can be modified by memory. Memory can transform the incomplete (happiness) into the complete and the complete (pain) into the incomplete'.

This can only mean that the operation of memory consists in restoring possibility to the past, in somehow making possible what seemed definitively fulfilled. Every time we truly remember something – that is, when the past suddenly bursts into our memory with such intensity that it seems we have never experienced it before – at that moment, the past is not something immutable and dead, but we perceive it again as possible and alive, as if it could have been – indeed, could still be – otherwise.

It is to this form of memory and its sudden epiphanies in a material object that Proust dedicated his work. This means dislodging the past from its place in chronology and situating it in the present, where we did not expect to find it: 'it (the past) hides itself outside its scope and reach, in some material object [. . .] of which we had no suspicion. It is chance that decides whether we will encounter this object before we die'. The object in question – which comes into being posthumously, so to speak, in a sort of remnant or relic – can be a biscuit, a piece of a white wall or a loose brick in the pavement; but it can also be a photograph.

Brassaï has reconstructed the particular, passionate attention that Proust devoted to the photographs of friends and loved ones. When he was twenty-two, a young Swiss man he had fallen in love with, Edgar Albert, gave him a portrait of himself on which he had written a verse by Rossetti: 'Look at my face: my name is Might have been; I am also called No more, Too late, Farewell'. The phrase must have struck him so profoundly that Proust made it the business of his conception of memory. Recalling Madeleine Lemaire's *salon* and the parties had there, he writes that 'every time, to evoke her, I contemplate one of those parties in the trembling, opaque depths of my memory', he seems to hear her voice saying: 'Take my visage, try, if you can, to look at it in the face; my name is what *might have been* and was not' (Brassaï, p. 39). Princess Bibesco recalls that, during a conversation in which happiness was in question, Proust 'began to expound at length on what seemed to me to be a eulogy of failure, to what could have been and was not' (ibid., p. 41).

In what way can a recollection, which, like a photograph, seems to irrevocably fix what has been, contain the essence of what could have been otherwise? It is not so much a question of failure, as of the specific performance of involuntary memory. Distinguishing between memory [*memoria*] (*Gedächtnis*) and recollection [*ricordo*] (*Erinnerung*), Theodor Reik has written that while the former is essentially conservative, because it aims at preservation of the impressions received, the second is destructive, because it aims to break them down. If memory can be compared to an archive, which preserves what has already been in its irreparably concluded state, recollection breaks down the walls of the archive and captures the past at the point where it first emerges into the present with all its possibilities – including of what is not being recalled. Recollection is, that is, constitutively forgetful of what it recalls. The feeling of 'déjà vu' that accompanies it is nothing more than the remnant or shadow that recollection casts into the past, just as dreams only exist for us in the moment when we recall them upon waking.

5. If we consider the activity that anthropologists define as 'cumulative history' – that is, the societies in which we live, as distinguished from primitive societies or 'stationary history' – dedicated to the transmission of the past, we see that it primarily involves the immense accumulation, preservation and transmission of remnants. Not only archives – public or private – museums of all species and genres, the 'treasures' of churches and crowns, antique shops, cities themselves completely transformed and turned into 'historic centres', but also the impressive system of educational institutions and schools of all grades and levels, from primary schools to universities, would be unthinkable if there were no remnants of the past. Whether it is – as in the discipline that

defines itself today as 'archaeology of human remains' – actual secular relics, which archaeologists exhume from their tombs to glean information about the social and religious hierarchies to which they belonged, or even just old, innocuous ornaments, the variety and quantity of these remains is such that it defies any attempt at exhaustive cataloguing. In any case, however, a society can only be defined as 'historical' if it accumulates, preserves and seeks – since it is not always successful in so doing – to transmit these remains. If we imagine that the remains disappear or – as happens in societies with a stationary history – are reduced to a few sacred objects, then culture as we know it ceases to exist.

It goes without saying that the transmission of the remnants of the past involves a spiritual operation capable of bringing them back to life – and how this can happen is, today, less and less evident. Indeed, there are many signs that suggest that our relation with the past has been undergoing a lasting crisis for some time now, the outcome of which is far from easy to predict. The apparatuses occupied with transmitting the remnants seem to be circling the void to such an extent that even the most sensitive intellectuals have seriously considered the possibility of having to prepare to survive culture. Benjamin was thus able to write that what the past must first and foremost be saved from is that aspect of its tradition that considers it as a 'legacy' or 'heritage' to be transmitted (Benjamin, I.3, p. 1242). The history of culture, he added, 'increases the weight of the treasures that burden humanity, but does not give it the strength to shake them off and thereby take them in hand', that is, to be able to use them (II.2, p. 478). Once the remnants of the past are conceived of as 'cultural assets', the inevitable consequence is that their management is entrusted to an economy, that is, to a calculation of profits and losses, of what is saved and preserved and what is destroyed or put up for sale. However, the problem of remnants and their transmission is not only not eliminated, but precisely because they are 'assets' whose price can be estimated, they now become even more unwieldy. Do the remains of the past have economic value because we believe it is right to preserve them, or is the opposite true? And what is a remnant, if we try to think of it as such?

The perfectly serious remark with which Moritz Steinschneider, one of the founders of Jewish studies, responded to those who asked him what the purpose of his studies was is memorable: 'The only thing we can do is ensure Judaism a decent funeral'. It is possible that today this bitter diagnosis must be extended to the history of western culture as a whole.

6. Tradition means 'delivery'. Chaim Nachman Bialik has distinguished two elements in Jewish tradition: the Halachah, that is, doctrine in its codified legal form, 'ironclad, pedantic, severe, an expression of rigour', and the Aggadah, the non-legal part of tradition, which takes the form of stories and parables, 'light and indulgent, an expression of mercy'. Benjamin took up this distinction to define Kafka's peculiar position relative to tradition, of which his work represents, so to speak, a sickness. While, for Bialik, Halachah and Aggadah are 'one thing, like two faces of the same creature', and Halachah is only the crystallization and final result of Aggadah, and Aggadah is Halachah restored to its fluidity, Benjamin, on the other hand, decisively opposes truth in its

Aggadic consistency, that is, in its transmissibility, to truth as law in itself, regardless of its 'deliverability'. In an age that had lost the Aggadic consistency of truth and in which most people tried to hold on to truth at all costs, more or less cheaply giving up on delivering it and passing it on, 'what is truly brilliant about Kafka is that he tried something completely new: he sacrificed truth in order to save its transmissibility, its Aggadic element' (Benjamin and Scholem, p. 272).

It is likely that our culture is still suffering from the sickness described by Kafka – and, if possible, in an even more acute phase. It is split between a transmission that has no truth to transmit and a truth that has lost all capacity to be transmitted, in stories and tales that no longer have anything to teach and precepts that are as authoritative as they are inapplicable. This means that we live in an age in which the problem of the remnant has achieved its critical mass. The accumulations of the remnants of the past in archives and registers is matched by a substantial loss of memory; the incapacity to use and transmit the remnants and memories is matched by the excessive growth of another, more disturbing figure of the remnant, that which must be by all means eliminated and destroyed. And it is precisely on this obscure, unwatchable remnant – the 'waste' that no landfill can contain, and no recycling can completely reintegrate into use – that industrial and post-industrial society seems to be irrevocably shipwrecked. The apocalyptic cipher of this shipwreck is the production of indestructible waste: nuclear waste, whose lifespan exceeds by hundreds of thousands of years the probable survival of the humanity that should take charge of it.

7. The concept of the remnant is tightly connected to that of salvation in a theological doctrine that is an essential part of Jewish and Pauline messianism. In the prophetic tradition, the 'remnant' (*shear*, *scherit*, in the Septuagint *kataleimma*, *kataleiphthen* and *hypoleimma*) refers, in fact, to Israel as the subject of eschatological salvation. The term appears in Isaiah from the beginning of his vision, referring to the devastation of Jerusalem, whose people have abandoned their God: 'If the Lord of Hosts had not left us a remnant, we would already be like Sodom, like Gomorrah' (Isaiah 1:9). But the exemplary passage is in Isaiah's messianic prophecy, 10:20–22: 'In that day the remnant of Israel and the survivors of the house of Jacob will no longer rely on those who struck them, but they will rely on the Lord, the Holy One of Israel, in faithfulness. The remnant, the remnant of Jacob, will return to the mighty God. For though your people, O Israel, will be like the sand of the sea, only a remnant will be saved'. Shortly before, the idea of a remnant is contained in the very name of the son that Yahweh announces to Isaiah: *Shear iasub*, 'a remnant will return' (or be saved – return and salvation are intimately connected in Judaism). In the prophecy against the King of Assyria, the salvation of Jerusalem is again linked to the announcement of a remnant: 'For out of Jerusalem shall go forth a remnant, they that escape from Mount Zion. The zeal of the Lord shall do this' (37:32). And it is to this 'remnant' that the prophet addresses himself to announce victory over false gods and the salvation to come: 'Hear me, O house of Jacob, and all the remnant of Israel, you who are taken from the womb, carried from birth [. . .]. As I have done before, so I will sustain you, carry you and save you' (46:3–4).

In Micah (4:7), too, the messianic announcement concerns a remnant, which God himself constitutes as such: 'On that day', says the Lord, 'I will gather the lame, I will assemble the scattered and those whom I have treated harshly. I will make the lame a remnant, and the scattered a strong nation'. And Amos (5:15), warning that those who await the Day of the Lord, that 'it will be darkness and not light for them', because 'there will be wailing in all the streets', announces aporetically, nonetheless, the salvation of a remnant: 'Despise evil and love good. Observe justice, which is at the door, and perhaps the Lord, the God of hosts, will have mercy on the remnant of Joseph'. And when, in Ezekiel, the Lord announces Israel's end and sends his angels to mercilessly exterminate 'old men, young men, girls, children and women', it is the idea of a remnant that the prophet opposes to him: 'Ah! Lord, will you destroy the remnant of Israel, pouring out your fury on Jerusalem [. . .] do you really want to destroy the remnant of Israel?' (9:8–11, 13).

8. It is this prophetic tradition that Paul takes up and develops in his Letter to the Romans (11:5–26). According to his characteristic radicalization of messianism, the remnant is no longer something that concerns the future but a present reality, which coincides with the messianic 'now': 'in the time of the now (*en to nyn kairoi*) by the election of grace a remnant has been brought forth (*leimma* [. . .] *gegonen*)'. Contradicting Isaiah's prophecy ('only a remnant will be saved'), Paul, who sees in the end of time the pleromatic moment when God 'will be all in all' (*panta en pasin*), announces with equal firmness – even if it is a 'mystery' (*Mysterion* *touto*) – that 'all Israel will be saved' (*pas Israel sothesetai*: 11:26).

The messianic significance of this remnant is misunderstood if, as most interpreters do, it is seen as a numerical portion, that is, the part of Israel that survives the eschatological catastrophe and thus constitutes a kind of bridge between ruin and salvation. But even the remnant cannot simply coincide with Israel as the chosen people who survive the destruction of the nations. A careful reading of both the prophetic texts and the Pauline passages shows that the remnant is, rather, the consistency that Israel assumes when it is in immediate relation to the messianic event. That is, it does not coincide with either the whole or its part, but signifies the impossibility of the coincidence of the whole and the part with each other. If the relic is a part that claims to be valid for the whole, the relation between the whole and the part undergoes a further complication. The remnant is a whole that constitutes itself as a part and a part that exceeds the whole of which it is a fraction. On the last day – that is, at the decisive moment – the chosen people – and, perhaps, every people – necessarily present themselves as a remnant, as not-all. This is the 'mystery' that Paul announces to the Romans.

9. In Lurianic Kabbalah, the doctrine takes an unexpected turn. It shifts from the people of Israel to their God. God's first act (of *En-Sof*, as the Kabbalists call the divinity in its mysterious origin) is neither an act of revelation nor a creation, it is rather a contraction and concealment, not a proceeding of God outside of himself, but a withdrawal into himself (*contraxerit se a se ipso in se ipsum*, according to the vivid formula of

Knorr von Rosenroth in his *Revealed Kabbalah*). Since God is everywhere, in order for a world to exist and be created out of nothing, he had to concentrate and sink into himself, in some way becoming nothing. This intradivine process is called *tzimtzum*, 'contraction' or 'withdrawal', and is in some ways a kind of exile of God into himself ('the idea of Tzimtzum', wrote Scholem, 'is the deepest symbol of exile thinkable': p. 271).

This is where the idea of a remnant appears. According to Luria, God's withdrawal into his nothingness leaves a remnant (*reshimu*), comparable – but this is obviously only an image – to the residue of wine or oil that remains in a bottle after it has been emptied. How should we think about this remnant? Is it still something divine, or is it a void of God? 'One could argue', writes Scholem, emphasizing the aporias implicit in Lurianic doctrine, 'that this *reshimu* is still constituted by the same divine substance; but one could also emphasize the fact that the substance of the *En-Sof* has disappeared here, so that the result of this process must be found outside God' (ibid., p. 274). It is easy to understand why this conception, which presupposed an empty and yet somehow divine 'remnant' of God, was judged blasphemous as soon as it appeared.

In the subsequent developments of Lurianic doctrine, the movement of God's exile within himself is only a prelude to his revelation in creation. If we consider, however, the *Tzimtzum* in itself, we find ourselves faced, on the one hand, with a God who has contracted within himself to the point of disappearing and, on the other, with a primordial space in which he is present at the stage of a 'remnant'. How can we conceive of such a space, such a world before the world – assuming that it makes sense to speak here of a world? What does it mean to exist in the mode of a remnant? And what is the relation of God to his remnant and of the remnant to God?

10. If we accept Scholem's suggestion that *Tzimtzum* is, in truth, a symbol of exile, of the *galut* that defines the condition of Jews in the world, then it is possible that the doctrine contains the metaphysical paradigm of Jewish existence. 'The righteous are in their graves and the prophets have fallen asleep, and we, we have been driven from our land, Zion has been taken from us and we have nothing left but God and his Torah', reads the *Syriac Apocalypse* of Baruch (LXXXV, 3). Since God has always withdrawn into himself and leaves only a remnant to exist, the people he has chosen and scattered into exile can in turn exist only in residual form, assuming from time to time a foreign identity and language, in relation to which the Jew nevertheless always places himself in a position of remnant. Exile is therefore not a contingent historical situation, which Zionism has sought at all costs to erase, but a metaphysical condition that defines and determines the possibilities of existence in history. As Amnon Raz-Krakotzkin has pointed out, the idea of exile was formed even before the second destruction of the Temple in 70 CE and presupposes that God exiled himself from sacred history, which ended with the Bible and, deprived of the divine presence, became purely profane and without any meaning other than anecdotal (Raz-Krakotzkin, p. 44). Not only with regard to the messianic event, but according to its essence, Israel is always *shear Israel* or *sherit Josep*, it is always not-all and in excess of any identity. For this

reason, in the words of Hosea (cited by Paul), Israel is constitutively a non-people ('I will call their name not-my-people, for you are not my people and I am not for you': 1:9) and, at the same time and precisely for this reason, as a non-people, the Jews 'shall be called children of the living God' (2:3). And for this reason, Shlomo Pines has observed, while the Jews' belonging to the cultures in which they lived and whose language they adopted is a historical fact, even if it has not been integrated into their consciousness, Jewish identity as such is a problem and not a given. Israel is the people who live as a remnant in a world that is itself only a remnant of God.

11. Like any genuine theological concept, the concept of a remnant is a concept of the philosophy of history. It expresses not only the non-coincidence between the whole and the part, but also that of the *olam hazzeh* – the time from creation to the end of the world – and the *olam habba*, the aeon to come, between the no longer and the not yet, between the past and the future. This time that remains between the two aeons is precisely historical time, which is neither the measurable chronological series nor timeless and immeasurable eternity. History is this remnant, which prevents the two aeons from coinciding and passing into one another and leaves open between them the space of human existence.

It is here that the messianic idea of a remnant merges with that which defines historical time. According to Scholem's critique of Jewish messianism, living in a time that remains does not mean existing in a state of deferral and waiting, but experiencing every moment as 'the small part through which the Messiah enters', as such unassignable to a moment in chronology, which is in fact interrupted and broken at every point. Messianic time is not the end of time, that is, a portion – the last – of chronological time, but the time of the end, a time that contracts and begins to end and, while not outside of it, does not coincide with chronological time, because it incessantly transforms it from within. The time that, in this sense, remains for us to live at every moment is the only time we can grasp as our own, the only time we have.

12. In Indian tradition, leftover foods are considered impure. Those who eat leftovers are contaminated by them and commit a sin from which they must purify themselves. 'May the waters purify me from having eaten remnants (*ucchistam*)', – recites a prayer from the *Taittiriyaranyaka*, – 'from forbidden foods, from all my evil deeds and from having accepted gifts from evil men' (Malamoud, p. 20). And yet there are remnants, those from sacrifice, which constitute pure food par excellence.

From the remnants of food offered to the gods in the sacrificial oblation the sacrifice takes three meatballs each time for the Brahmins he has invited to the ceremony. 'Good men who feed on the remains of sacrifice are free from all contamination; but those who cook food for their own use and consumption are sinners and feed on sin' (*Bhagavadgītā*, III, 13). This also applies to the leftovers left by the master, which the disciple must eat religiously as if they were the remains of an oblation. This particular status of remnants is not limited to the sphere of food. The remnant is also the secret engine of the cycle of rebirths produced by *karma*. The good and bad actions of each individual do not balance each other out, but there remains a surplus or residue (*anusaya*), which determines reincarnation and thus keeps the endless mechanism of births in motion. It is this remnant of *karma* that the *samniasyn*, the 'renunciate', seeks to escape, but it is this same remnant that ensures those who have acted well a series of good rebirths that will enable them to reach heaven. It is not surprising that something like a remnant is also found in the sphere of language. According to the *Aitareya Upaniṣad*, *vac*, the word, does not coincide with the syllables that form it, but is like a remnant (*ucchisyate*) that exceeds them. The syllables that make up a word are never the whole, just as *vac* is not the sum of its parts, but a remnant in relation to them. As the author of the *Aitareya* vividly writes: 'the syllable – *aksasram* – is trisyllabic, the word, *vac*, is a single syllable' (Malamoud, p. 295). This can also be expressed by saying that what the word means – the semantic element – is a remnant of its sound or phonetic reality.

In this sense Malamoud can assert that the concept of the remnant occupies a fundamental place in Brahamanic doctrines. 'A quantity of matter or actions is not normally consumed in its entirety; the operations to which it is subjected do not lead to a definitive result: a remnant remains, ambiguous, but with the characteristic of not being inert, but active' (ibid., p. 38). We can therefore understand why the *Atharvaveda* collection states: 'On the remnant (*uchiste*) are founded name and form, on the remnant is founded the world. In the remnant, Indra and Agni, everything, are concentrated [. . .]. Being and non-being, both are in the remnant, death, vigour, Prajapati [. . .]. The inhaled and exhaled breath, sight, hearing, the fact that things are imperishable, even the fact that they perish: from the remnant were born all the gods who are in heaven and who dwell in heaven' (ibid., p. 39).

13. Between 1803 and 1804, Hölderlin composed the hymn 'Andenken' (Memory), which was published in the *Musenalmanach* in 1808. As the title suggests, the five stanzas of the poem invoke in various ways something from the past – recent, as in the first stanza, which describes the landscape of France ('the beautiful Garonne / and the gardens of Bordeaux') that Hölderlin had travelled through a year earlier – or further back in time, as in the fourth stanza, 'friends' and Bellarmino, the recipient of the letters in *Hyperion* ('But where are the friends? Bellarmino / with his companion. . .'). In the last stanza, the French landscape is invoked once again, together with the sea 'that takes away / and gives memory' and love 'that tenaciously pursues the eyes'. At this point, the hymn abruptly ends with the verse: *Was bleibet aber, stiften die Dichter* ('what remains, the poets establish').

Hölderlin's intention is misunderstood if *Was bleibet* is understood as that which remains and will endure over time, i.e., the poet's work. Martin Heidegger fell into this error, at least initially, when he devoted his winter semester course in 1941–2 to the exegesis of the hymn. 'The discourse', he writes before turning to his analysis of the stanzas, 'focuses here on founding, on the foundation of something future, not on the memory of things run their course. It speak of what remains, not of what passes and is past. If we already reflect here on the fact that in Hölderlin's poems everything comes together only in the closing lines, then the relationship between the closing lines of the poem and its title, which must always characterize the whole, becomes completely enigmatic' (Heidegger 1982, p. 25). At the end of the course, commenting on the final verse, Heidegger further elaborates on his interpretation. The thought – the memory (*Andenken*) – that is at stake in the hymn is directed both towards the past and towards 'what is to come'. Thinking back and forward (*zurück- und vordenkende*), memory shows its belonging to destiny: 'this thinking belonging is the initial essence of memory'.

At this point, the philosopher introduces a new element, which shifts the interpretation in a less obvious direction. 'In order to establish what remains, the poet himself must be a remnant (*ein bleibender*); he must be capable of one thing: to remain in the much that remains to be endured over time and to be said in song' (ibid., p. 163). What is decisive here is no longer the poet's situation between past and future, between what has been and the canto to come, but the fact that the poet himself must place himself in a position of remnant, must be only 'something that remains'. Relative to what?

14. It has long been observed that, in Hölderlin's late hymns, the gods appear in the atheological figure of departure. The correction of the last verse of 'Dichterberuf', *solange der Gott nicht fehlet*, 'as long as God is not missing', to *solange bis Gottes Fehl hilft*, 'as long as God's absence helps', is not simply 'ironic', as Beissner suggests, but inaugurates the new and unprecedented relation with the divine that characterizes the late Hölderlin. The time in which the poet loves and loses himself is a 'time of deprivation' (*dürftiger Zeit*),

in which 'the Most High turns away / and nothing immortal can be seen in heaven / or on the green earth' (Patmos) and men 'without gods' (*Götterlosen*) wander in the sacred night 'as if in sleep' (*wie Schlummer*). It is no coincidence that the extreme figure of this departure of the gods is Christ ('the last of your lineage') – that is, a divine person in whom, according to Paul's dictum, God emptied himself of his divinity (*eauton ekenosen*: Letter to the Philippians, 2:7). Christ – curiously assimilated to Dionysius – is what remains once the gods have withdrawn from the world (thus Dionysius is said to 'remain (*bleibet*) and the trace of the vanquished gods / brings back into darkness the godless men' (str. 9). All the final stanzas of 'Brot und Wein' (Hölderlin) can be read in the sense of a purely kenotic theology, in which God 'took the form of man / and ended and closed, consoling, the heavenly feast' (str. 6).

The particular nature of this Hölderlinian poetic atheology cannot be understood, however, if we do not measure the distance that separates it from the kenotic theology of the twentieth century. For while in the latter, the withdrawal of the divine and existence in a world without God take on a dark and decidedly tragic aspect, Hölderlin instead experiences the absence of God as a condition that is ultimately serene and, so to speak, somnambulistically happy. Hence the paradoxical formulations such as 'the absence that helps' and, in the *Note* to the translation of *Oedipus*, the idea of a 'betrayal of sacred species' ('man forgets himself and God and turns away, but in a sacred way, like a traitor'). This seemingly contradictory condition sometimes seems to foreshadow a future return of the gods, and it is in this sense that interpreters read it – and yet, as if to refute the interpretation, the hymn dedicated to *Mnemosyne* peremptorily states that 'we do not want to look either forward or backward'. We need to think of the time in question here beyond the distinction between past and future, as that time – the messianic – that remains between them, and likewise the divine not as something irrevocably past or yet to come, but as continuously and timelessly present in the figure of a remnant.

The anti-tragic and joyful nature of this experience of the divine is evident in Hölderlin's last poems, many of which are signed with the pseudonym Scardanelli, in which, in the simple description of the changing seasons, human life now appears 'as an image of divinity', whose 'perfection is without lament'. The fact that these poems are usually classified as works of 'madness' simply means that, at the time they were composed, a theology such as that expressed in them could only be conceived at this price.

15. It is possible, then, that the language of poetry is not a special language, but something like a remnant of language, that language is, in the words of Arendt, that which 'remains' par excellence. Critics have noted the particular difficulty of the language of Hölderlin's later works, in which the isolation of words and extreme parataxis make it almost impossible to understand the meaning with certainty. It is this collapse of syntax and the normal semantic connections of language that made the translations of Sophocles, to which Hölderlin had dedicated his final efforts, unserviceable and almost laughable in the eyes of Goethe and Schiller. This is even more true of Celan's poetry, in which an attentive

reader such as Primo Levi could discern only 'inarticulate babbling, something like a death rattle', in any case 'not communication and not even language proper' (Levi, p. 637). In both cases, it is as if the communicative functions that make language (German) comprehensible in common usage were removed and deactivated one by one. The language of poetry is what *remains* after these functions have been progressively eliminated or reduced to their lowest limit: *even when all the operations of language have been deactivated, something always remains and this remnant is poetry*. It is possible that it corresponds to an original or Adamic state of language, when the name had not yet fallen into meaning; the fact remains, however, that it appears to us today as a remnant.

The illustrious vernacular Dante describes in *De vulgari eloquentia* is also similar; this is not a language that can be identified or assigned to this or that city, but only what remains when the fourteen vernaculars spoken in the various regions and cities of Italy have been purified of their characteristics and imperfections. The 'illustrious, courtly and cardinal vernacular' is not another language but what remains when the municipal vernaculars have been 'bent inward and outward', 'incessantly uprooting from the Italian forest' the 'thorny bushes' that disfigure it. The 'panther' that Dante has set about hunting, which 'sends its scent everywhere and appears nowhere', is precisely that language that no city can claim as its own, what remains after the functions and modes through which speakers appropriate their words have been rendered inoperative. The language of poetry is the incommunicable that remains after all communication has been suspended and deactivated, the unutterable remnant that exceeds every idiom and every linguistic exchange – in this sense, in the words of Giovanni Pascoli, the dead language that inhabits and resists in every language we call living.

16. The idea of a 'language that remains' or a 'remnant of language' is also central to philosophical tradition. In his treatise on *Categories*, Aristotle lists, in an apparently exhaustive manner, the ten fundamental forms of what is said (of the *legomena*): substance, quality, quantity, place, time, relation, action, suffering, having, lying. In a now famous essay, Benveniste showed that these categories, which in the history of philosophy have been interpreted as the ways being is given, actually correspond to the fundamental structures of the Greek language. But even the ancient commentators, when defining the subject of a book, had realized that the philosopher did not intend to deal only with entities or only with language, but with entities as they are designated through terms. Ontology and logic are, in this sense, inseparable. But it is precisely from this close ontological implication of being and language – whereby being is what is said and language says what is (or is not) each time – that philosophy defines its task and its specific performance. Philosophy seeks, in fact, to grasp the implication of being and language, to say neither simply things nor language, but that very connection between language and the world, which constitutes language as language and language being as being. The word that expresses and explains this implication cannot be a denoting discourse within language, which says something about something – rather, it must express language itself insofar as it expresses being, and being insofar as it is expressed in language, without resorting to any metalanguage that would allow it to take language as an object.

Hence, for Plato, the difficulty of talking about the idea: this, being anonymous, can only be defined homonymously with respect to sensible entities ('the circle itself', 'the horse itself'. . .) as the 'thing itself' that is at stake in any discourse about them. Similarly, Aristotle, after defining essence as the presupposition on which everything is predicated, but which itself is not predicated of anything, must then try to grasp this remainder of language that always escapes in the past beyond categories such as the 'being that was' (*ti en einai*) in question in each of them. Here, thought must take measure of anomalous terms that do not seem to denote anything and yet are always implicit in the fact that we are talking or have talked about something and remain, in this sense, sayable and unsaid in every discourse.

Philosophy could be defined from this perspective as the search for that part of language that 'remains' when all meaningful propositions – all *doxai*, opinions that say something about something – have been said (or are supposed to have been said). Like poetry, it is a 'language that remains' or 'a remnant of language'.

17. Scholastic philosophy refers to this remainder as a transcendental. Transcendental (*transcendentia*) or super-transcendental (*supertranscendentia*) terms are those whose meaning is identical to 'being' (*ens*) and which, despite being immanent in every category and every discourse, cannot be reduced to them ('one (*unum*)', 'true (*verum*)', 'thing (*res*)', 'something (*aliquid*)'). For this reason, in the history of philosophy, the

problem of transcendentals tends to coincide with that of the object of metaphysics or first philosophy. What is essential here is not the distinction between those who believe that the object of metaphysics is 'being *qua* being', 'God', the thing or 'something', but rather the problematic status of these terms, which, although always already stated and presupposed in every discourse, cannot themselves be 'said' and unambiguously defined. The transcendental designates, that is, a part or, rather, a margin of language in which it ceases to denote and yet still remains in some way a language (even if the question of whether this remainder of language is still something linguistic is decisive here in every sense).

When Kant, identifying the transcendental as the only possible object of philosophy, believed he had found a new stronghold for it, he remained instead a tributary of an ancient scholastic tradition. His 'concept of an object in general' and 'noumenon = X', about which it is impossible to say whether they are something or nothing, leave unanswered the only question that matters: whether language (the 'transcendentals', such as the language that remains to philosophy) is or is not something exclusively linguistic. In this way, the idea, whose existence Plato still affirmed alongside the sensible, becomes a space that must remain empty beyond the limits of verifiable knowledge alone – that is, scientific knowledge. The division of philosophy into logic, which deals with the formal correctness of denoting propositions, and metaphysics, which insists on speaking, so to say, in a vacuum, betrays the impossibility of language to coincide with itself completely. In truth, language, for the simple fact that it cannot express itself and must nevertheless try to do so, cannot coincide with itself, cannot be whole. It is this discrepancy, this 'not being-all' of language, that philosophy deals with. And if, before transmitting any tradition, humans must necessarily transmit language, poetry and philosophy take on the transmission of that remainder of language that exceeds the scope of opinion and the communication of messages (which is why Wittgenstein could say, for example, 'in philosophy, I have no opinions').

18. *Hypostasis* in Greek means residue, sediment (in Hippocrates, urine deposits; in Aristotle excrement as nutritional residue). This is not how we understand the term 'remnant' here. Rather, it expresses the impossibility of something – of being or of language – coinciding with itself and with something else, that is, a principle stubbornly resisting identity. Émile Meyerson observed that the sign = in an equation can have many meanings ('is equal to', 'can be replaced', 'has the same properties', etc.), but in no case can it express absolute identity. The identity between two terms joined by the equal sign can therefore only be partial, otherwise it would contradict Leibniz's principle of indiscernibles, according to which no two entities exist in nature that are distinct only in number, because in this case it would be impossible to distinguish them. This can also be expressed by saying that being and language are never identical to themselves but are constitutively in a position of remainder with respect to any identity. The remnant, in this sense, is never a residue or an inert substance, but something that is produced in the relation between two terms that tend, without success, to identify with each other.

Both formulas define pantheism for the young Hölderlin: *en kai pan*, one and all. Or the genuinely

Spinozian *Deus sive natura*. They do not mean 'one = all' or 'God = nature', because what is to be considered in them is precisely the meaning of the particles *kai* ('and') and *sive* ('or'). The divine is not God in himself or in his identity with nature, but his *sive*, his ever-changing and naturalizing – his 'birth' – in the infinite ways that constitute nature. The divine is, that is, the remnant that is constantly produced between God and nature, which ensures that their relation is not inert identity, but life.

Let us now consider the Pauline formula according to which 'God is all in all' (*pas en pasin*: 1 Cor 15:28). It cannot signify the tautology that the whole is equal to all things. God is wholly alone like the remnant that is produced in the impossibility of everything and every language coinciding with itself, in their necessarily being not-all. Between the one substance and its infinite modes, God is constitutively the remnant. And this is the only sensible way to understand pantheism.

19. Even the human cannot coincide with themselves; they cannot be 'all', that is, wholly human. Let us consider anthropogenesis, or the becoming *sapiens* (*sapiens loquendi*, meaning the one who knows how to speak, not simply the one who speaks) of the primate of the genus *Homo*. Humanity cannot be conceived of as something that has totally absorbed and captured within itself the animality that preceded it. Between the animal and the speaking being there is necessarily a remnant, and only this remnant is truly human. This remnant is language, not as a system of signs in some way similar to animal languages, but insofar as it constitutively exceeds them. For this reason, anthropogenesis is not an event that occurred once and for all *in illo tempore*, but rather a process that is always ongoing and must remain so; for this reason, human language continues to mutate and evolve historically, without knowing where. If humans claimed to have realized and eliminated their animal nature, if language, establishing itself as the achieved animal voice of *Homo sapiens*, presumed to perfectly express what has no words – that is, if a formally perfect language were possible once and for all – then not only would history come to a standstill, but the very terms 'man' and 'animal' would lose their meaning and, as seems to be happening today, we would no longer know what is human and what is inhuman. And like man, his history cannot be fulfilled, not because it lasts indefinitely, but, on the contrary, because it ends at every moment, it is always in a position of remainder between the endless abstraction of chronological time and the equally abstract idea of the end of time.

It is in this sense that Blanchot's statement that 'man is the indestructible that can be infinitely destroyed' should be understood. It does not mean that there is an essence in man that can never be completely destroyed; rather, it means that man is always on this side or beyond the human, always a remnant between man and non-man, between destruction and salvation, between what is saved and what is lost. An Arab legend attributes this explanation of the weeping of Iblis (the fallen angel of Islam) to the Sufi poet al-Hallaj: 'Iblis weeps for the world because he would like it to survive destruction, he weeps for the things that pass away and would like to bring them back to life, because he does not know that what remains is God's (*lilah al-baqi*)'.

20. What, in the end, remains? What remains of language? A short text by Italo Calvino dedicated to his friends as his 'spiritual testament' concludes with a series of broken phrases, hammered out almost breathlessly: 'the theme of memory expulsion of memory lost memory preserving and losing what is lost what one did not have what one had too late what we carry with us what does not belong to us living without carrying anything with us (the animal): perhaps we carry with us more the living for the work: we lose ourselves: there is the useless work: there is no longer me'.

It is possible to read this jumble of fragments as a meditation on 'what we carry with us' and what remains with us – and yet this remnant is defined only in negative terms and by hints. The memory, invoked at the beginning, is an 'expelled' and 'lost' memory, as if it were entrusted with the arduous, impossible task of 'preserving and losing what is lost'. The fact is that, both in individual and collective life, the mass of things and words that are lost, the waste of tiny, imperceptible events that are forgotten every day, is so vast that no archive and no memory could possibly contain their registers. And yet, what remains, that part of life and language that we save from ruin, has a special relation with what has been lost, stands in some way for it, speaks and responds on its behalf. The ultimate question is therefore not 'what did we have or miss?' nor 'what is saved?', but 'what remains?' – not as a fragment of the past, but as something new, emerging for the first time and breaking the fabric that memory and language weave and unravel at every moment. At that point, the salvation of what has been lost is in the perception of the unsalvageable, and what remains is an undecidable mixture of salvation and ruin. There is, that is, a tradition of what is lost, which runs parallel to that of what is saved and cuts it in several places – and it is precisely its immemorial ruin that defines the rank of what we manage to say and remember.

Only in this way can Paul's apparent contradiction in the Letter to the Romans ('only the remnant will be saved': 9:27; 'all Israel will be saved': 11:26) be reconciled, just as the apocalyptic confession 'we have nothing left but God and the Torah' reveals its true meaning. What does it mean to live on what remains? Does it mean that all that remains is lost? Or does it rather mean that the remnant is not only a part of what is lost, but its most intimate and obscure core – that what the remnant guards as its most precious possession is nothing other than the need of the forgotten to remain, *as such*, unforgettable? That, to paraphrase al-Hallaj's saying, 'what is lost belongs to God'?

Bibliography

Althaus, Paul. *Die letzten Dinge*. Gütersloh: Bertelsmann, 1922.

Arendt, Hannah. *Essays in Understanding*. New York: Harcourt Brace, 1994.

Arendt, Hannah. *Quaderni e Diari*. Milan: Neri Pozza, 2007.

Ballanche, Pierre-Simon. *Palingénésie sociale: prolégomènes*, vol. IV. Paris: Bureau de l'Encyclopédie des connaissances utiles, 1833.

Barth, Karl. *Der Römerbrief*. Bern: G. A. Bäschlin, 1919.

Barth, Karl. *Kirchliche Dogmatik*, vol. II/1. Zürich: Zollikon, 1958.

Benjamin, Walter. *Gesammelte Schriften*, vols. I–V. Edited by Rolf Tiedemann and Hermann Schweppenhäuser. Frankfurt am Main: Suhrkamp, 1974–82.

Benjamin, Walter, and Gershom Scholem. *Briefwechsel 1933–1940*. Frankfurt am Main: Suhrkamp, 1980.

Bergson, Henri-Louis. *Matière et mémoire*. Paris: PUF, 1939.

Bergson, Henri-Louis. *Le possible et le réel.* Edited by Alexandre Bouaniche and Frédéric Worms. Paris: PUF, 2011.

Bloch, Marc. *Apologie pour l'histoire ou métier d'historien.* 1st ed. 1949. Paris: A. Colin, 1993.

Brassaï (Gyula Halász). *Marcel Proust sous l'emprise de la photographie.* Paris: Gallimard, 1997.

Burgess, Richard W. 'Apologetic and Chronography'. In *Julius Africanus und die christliche Weltchronistik*, edited by Martin Wallraff. Berlin–New York: de Gruyter, 2006.

Burkhardt, Johannes. *Die Entstehung des modernen Jahrhundertrechnung.* Göppingen: Kummerle, 1971.

Cartari, Vincenzo. *Imagini delli Dei de gl'Antichi.* Milan: Luni Editrice, 2013.

Caruth, Cathy. *Unclaimed Experience: Trauma, Narrative, and History.* Baltimore: Johns Hopkins University Press, 1996.

Coarelli, F. *Il foro romano: Periodo arcaico.* Rome: Edizione Quasar, 1983, pp. 199–226.

Derrida, J. *Introduction à l'Origine de la Géométrie de Husserl.* Paris: PUF, 1962.

Dognini, C. *Mundus: Etruria e oriente in un'istituzione romana.* Galatina: Congedo Editore, 2001.

Du Jardin, L. '*Mundus*, *Roma quadrata* e *Lapis niger*', *Rendiconti della Pontificia Accademia Romana di Archeologia* 6 (1930), pp. 47–76.

Dumézil, G. *La religion romaine archaïque.* Paris: Payot, 1966.

Evangelisti, F. 'Una congruenza lessicale latino-indiana (a proposito del *mundus* sotterraneo)', in *Studi in onore di Vittore Pisani.* Rome: Paideia, 1969.

Foucault, M. *Les mots et les choses: Une archéologie des sciences humaines*. Paris: Gallimard, 1966.

Foucault, M. *L'Archéologie du savoir*. Paris: Gallimard, 1969.

Hegel, G. W. F. *Lezioni sulla filosofia della storia*. Edited by G. Bonacina and L. Sichirollo. Rome–Bari: Laterza, 2003.

Heidegger, M. *Der Zeitbegriff in der Geschichtswissenschaft*. Leipzig: J. A. Barth, 1916.

Heidegger, M. *Sein und Zeit*. Halle: Niemeyer, 1927.

Heidegger, M. *Vom Wesen des Grundes*. Halle: Niemeyer, 1929.

Heidegger, M. *Zur Sache des Denkens*. Tübingen: Niemeyer, 1969.

Heidegger, M. *Hölderlins Hymne 'Andenken'*. Frankfurt am Main: Klostermann, 1982.

Husserl, E. *Husserliana*. Edited by W. Biemel, vol. VI. The Hague: M. Nijhoff, 1954.

Hippolytus. 'Su Cristo e l'anticristo', in *L'anticristo*, vol. I: *Il nemico dei tempi finali*, edited by G. L. Potestà and M. Rizzi. Milan: Fondazione Lorenzo Valla–Mondadori, 2005.

Jacoby, F. 'Über die Entwicklung der griechischen Historiographie', *Klio* 9 (1909), pp. 80–123.

Kaplan, M. 'De la dépouille à la relique: formation du culte des saints à Byzance du Ve au XIIe siècle', in *Les reliques: Objets, cultes, symboles*, edited by E. Bozóky and A.-M. Helvétius. Turnhout: Brepols, 1999.

Keizer, H. M. *Life Time Entirety: A Study of Aion in Greek Literature and Philosophy, the Septuagint and Philo*. Thesis, University of Amsterdam, 7 September 1999.

Koselleck, R. 'Krise'. In *Geschichtliche Grundbegriffe*, vol. VII, edited by W. Conze and R. Koselleck. Stuttgart: Klett-Cotta, 1992.

Le Bonniec, H. *Le culte de Cerès à Rome*. Paris: Klincksieck, 1958.

Levi, P. 'L'altrui mestiere', in *Opere*. Turin: Einaudi, 1990.

Lévy-Bruhl, H. 'Une notion confuse: le fait historique', in *Recherches philosophiques* V (1935–6).

Lorenz, O. *Die Geschichtswissenschaft in Hauptrichtungen und Aufgaben*. Berlin: W. Hertz, 1886.

Malamoud, C. *Cuocere il mondo: Rito e pensiero nell'India antica*. Milan: Adelphi, 1994.

Marrou, H. I. 'Morale et spiritualité chrétiennes dans le Pédagogue de Clément d'Alexandrie', in *Christiana tempora: mélanges d'histoire, d'archéologie, d'épigraphie et de patristique*. Rome: École Française de Rome, 1978.

Marrou, H. I. *Teologia della storia*, translated by R. Mazzariol. Milan: Jaca Book, 1979.

Mazzarino, S. *Il pensiero storico classico*. Bari: Laterza, 1966.

Mazzarino, S. *Fra Oriente e Occidente: Ricerche di storia greca arcaica*. Milan: Rizzoli, 1989, pp. 397–407.

Nichtweiss, B. *Erik Peterson: Neue Sicht auf Leben und Werk*. Freiburg im Breisgau: Herder, 1992.

Nietzsche, F. *Così parlò Zarathustra*. Milan: Adelphi, 1968.

Origen. *Traité des principes*, vols. 1–2. Edited by H. Crouzel and S. Simonetti. Paris: Cerf, 1980.

Overbeck, F. *Werke und Nachlass*, vol. VI.1: *Kirchenlexicon: Materialien, Christentum und Kultur*. Stuttgart–Weimar: Verlag Metzler, 1996.

Pasquali, G. *Storia della tradizione e critica del testo*. Florence: Le Monnier, 1952.
Péguy, C. *Clio: dialogo della storia con l'anima pagana*. Edited by Q. Antonelli and A. Prontera. Lecce: Milella, 1994.
Peter Lombard. *Collectanea in Epistulas Pauli, in Ep. II ad Thess*. In *Patrologia Latina*, 192.
Peterson, E. 'Offenbarung des Johannes und politisch-theologische Texte', in *Ausgewählte Schriften*, 4. Würzburg: Echter, 2004a.
Peterson, E. 'Lukasevangelium und Synoptica', in *Ausgewählte Schriften*, 5. Würzburg: Echter, 2004b.
Pisani, V. *Obiter scripta*, vol. III, in *Paideia* 17 (1962).
Platelle, H. 'Guibert de Nogent et le *De pignoribus sanctorum*: Richesses et limites d'une critique médiévale des reliques', in *Les reliques: Objets, cultes, symboles*, edited by E. Bozóky and A.-M. Helvétius. Turnhout: Brepols, 1999.
Poulet, G. *L'Espace proustien*. Paris: Gallimard, 1963.
Ramelli, I. *The Christian Doctrine of Apokatastasis*. Leiden–Boston: Brill, 2013.
Ranke, L. von. *Über die Epochen der neueren Geschichte: Vorträge dem Könige Maximilian II von Bayern gehalten*. Edited by A. Dove. Leipzig: Duncker & Humblot, 1906.
Raz-Krakotzkin, A. *Exil et souveraineté: judaïsme, sionisme et pensée binationale*. Paris: La fabrique, 2007.
Rose, H. J. 'The *mundus*', *Studi e materiali di storia delle religioni* 7 (1931), pp. 115–27.
Schmitt, C. *Der Nomos der Erde im Völkerrecht des 'Ius publicum Europaeum'*. Berlin: Duncker & Humblot, 1974.

Scholem, G. *Le grandi correnti della mistica ebraica*. Turin: Einaudi, 1997.

Solimano, G. 'Fedro V, 8'. In *Favolisti latini medievali e umanistici*, vol. VII, edited by Ferruccio Bertini. Università di Genova, Facoltà di Lettere e Filosofia, Genova, 1998.

Thomas, Y. 'La vérité, le temps, le juge et l'historien', *Le Débat* 102 (November–December 1998).

Vendryes, J. 'La famille du latin *mundus* "monde"', *Mémoires de la Société de Linguistique de Paris* 18.4 (1913).

Victricius. *De laude sanctorum*, in *Corpus Christianorum*, SL 64. Turnhout: Brepols, 1985.

Von den Brincken, Anna-Dorothee. 'Die lateinische Weltchronistik'. In *Mensch und Weltgeschichte*, edited by A. Randam. Salzburg–Munich: Pustet, 1969.

Wagenvoort, M. H. '*Initia Cereris*', in *Studies in Roman Literature, Culture and Religion*. Leiden: Brill Archive, 1956.

Warde-Fowler, W. '*Mundus patet*: 24 August, 5 October, 8 November', *Journal of Roman Studies* 2 (1912), pp. 25–33.

Weinstock, S. '*Mundus patet*', *Mitteilungen des deutschen archäologischen Instituts, Römische Abteilung* 45 (1930), pp. 111–23.